MW00816726

Five Pennies

Ten Rules to Successfully Build a Franchise Mega-Brand and Maximize System Profits

Lonnie Helgerson, CFE

12/29/16

To Laurie !

Wishing You greatest of success in franchising !!

All my best,

Lonnie Helgerson

"This book is an important piece of work for anyone who intends to make a living in the franchise community!"
- Sid Feltenstein, CFE, Past CEO & Chairman, A&W® and Long John Silver's®

"Lonnie has captured the true keys for franchising success. It is easy-to-read with great examples of BOTH the right way and the wrong way to grow a strong franchise brand. Poised to become the new textbook for aspiring franchisors, Five Pennies is a must-read!"
- Jeff Bevis, CFE, President & CEO, FirstLight Home Care®

"I can only say, that I certainly wish that I had an easy to read book like this when I was starting out - it would have eliminated some head, heart, and financial aches!"
- Mary Ellen Sheets, Founder, Two Men and a Truck®

Franchising is badly in need of information that works, that makes sense, which can guide us through these times of change in our industry. Best practices that teach us how to work—and also inspire us to understand why we work. Lonnie has done that with Five Pennies."
- Ken Hutcheson, CFE, CEO, U.S. Lawns®

"I have been in franchising since 1979. If I had been given a book like this back then, I could have shortened the learning curve. The book is an easy read with thought provoking ideas and great suggestions that can change an existing franchise system or quick start a new Franchisor."
- Mark J Johnson, CFE, CEO, Granite Transformations®

"Great read for anyone in the franchising business. It is clear, concise, and accurate of how to do build your brand the right way. Should be a mandatory read for everyone in the industry."
- Ron Randolph, CFE, Dewcor

"This book, with its considerable franchise related wisdom broken down in easy to read – as well as entertaining – "rules," promises to become a "go to" book for those starting out in franchising!"
- Rosemarie Hartnett, CFE, President & Co-Founder, Abrakadoodle®

"Five Pennies should be on everyone's read list who is thinking about franchising their business... Set the expectations right from the start and you will achieve long term success... Thanks for giving back to the industry!"
- Paul Wolbert, CFE, Vice President, U.S. Lawns®

"If you're serious about building a successful national brand, Five Pennies is an absolute must read! I highly recommend it as training material for all management and staff members - as the time spent reading this book is the best investment anyone working in franchising can make in their on-going education and their business."
- Ron Berger, CFE, Chairman and CEO of Figaro's Pizza®, Pizza Schmizza®, Nick'N'Willy's® & Sargo's Subs®

"Books about owning a franchise are plentiful. Books aimed at crafty people with good concepts on how to turn their local idea into a national brand and household name are harder to find. Lonnie has done it with Five Pennies."
- Jerrod Sessler, CFE, CEO of HomeTask®, Freggies®, Lawn Army®, Pet Butler® & Yellow Van Handyman®

"Five Pennies is THE field manual for building and growing a franchise brand with the right mindset and tools! Lonnie's knowledge and information can be applied to any franchise brand at any time for almost immediate results."

- Dan Monaghan, CFE, Director, Franchise Capital Corporation, and Co-Founder, WSI Internet Consulting

"Why anyone would think of starting a franchise without getting the best help available is beyond me. Why anyone would even consider thinking about it without reading Five Pennies, is simply INSANE!"
- Daniel Durney, CFE, Regional Franchise Development Expert

Published by Helgerson Franchise Group, LLC

www.HelgersonFranchiseGroup.com

Cover design by Marty Greenbaum, Greenbaum Marketing

www.GreenbaumMarketing.com

Master Editing by Mary Ann O'Connell, FranWise®

www.FranWise.com

Supplemental Editing by Dan Durney, CFE & Joan Painter, CFE

The Library of Congress has catalogued this Paperback Edition as follows:

First Edition

Five Pennies: Ten Rules to Successfully Build a Franchise Mega-Brand and Maximize System Profits

ISBN 978-0-9851810-1-7

Printed in the United States of America.

Table of Contents

Acknowledgments

This book is dedicated to my loving wife, Linette, and our four children Chandler, Ainsley, Hannah, and Nora. Without their enduring love, patience, and occasional prodding this book would not have been possible;

To my mother, Laverne Kraft, who always supported my entrepreneurial pursuits (in more ways than one at times) and my brother Phil for standing by my side as a friend and business partner through the years. To my former stepfather Ben Kraft who taught me that the key to happiness is being your own boss;

To the International Franchise Association (IFA), the International Institute for Franchise Education at the H. Wayne Huizenga School of Business and Entrepreneurship, Nova Southeastern University (IIFE), the Institute of Certified Franchise Executives (ICFE), and the school of hard knocks for all of the exceptional business and franchise training I have received over the years;

To Ron Rivett and Loren Steele, co-founders of Super 8 Motels®, who planted the franchising bug in my head all those years ago. To Cheryl Babcock and Jeff Rosenfeld who taught me the power of networking and business friendship. To my fishing/hunting buddy and fellow author Gerald W. Darnell for your insight and guidance;

And finally to all of my extended franchise family who have mentored and helped me throughout the years.

I am truly blessed to have all of you in my life!

Five Pennies VIP Club

I would like to thank the following people for their gracious assistance in making this book possible.

Paul Wolbert, CFE

Jeff Bevis, CFE

Ken Hutcheson, CFE

Marty Greenbaum

Mary Ann O'Connell

"Self-doubt is the biggest killer of success. The validation of your knowledge from others instills confidence and helps you achieve the seemingly impossible!"

> - Lonnie Helgerson, CFE

Definition

Franchise Mega-Brand

A franchise system that excels to greatness with a profitable and sustainable franchisee business model.

Introduction

"All men can see these tactics whereby I conquer, but what none can see is the strategy out of which victory is evolved."

Sun Tzu, The Art of War, 5th Century BC

This is Sun Tzu for Franchising

Every year *tens of thousands* of new franchisees open their doors for business and look to fulfill the American dream of success, and every year *hundreds* of new franchise companies announce their plans to be the next McDonald's®, SUBWAY® Restaurants, Marriott®, RE/MAX®, or Great Clips® and fail to reach that goal. Why?

Beyond the initial legal work, basic operations manual, some training and a fancy logo to get started, what does it really take to be a successful franchise brand? To start, let me put you in the right mindset.

Having a rapidly growing franchise company does not generate wealth and success. A franchisor's wealth and success are by-products of having wealthy and successful franchisees.

Makes complete sense doesn't it?

The ideas in this book will inspire you to adopt this as your *new* franchise brand strategic statement,

"Our wealth and success as a franchisor will be a <u>by-product</u> of developing wealthy and successful franchisees."

This book is not a step-by-step guide to franchising your business. It is a strategic guide based in 10 rules that will allow you to manage and grow your system into a franchise Mega-Brand.

As Sun Tzu said in his writings over 2,500 years ago the tactics you use may win you a few battles, but the unseen strategy you develop for your brand and franchisees is what will help you win the war and be successful.

If you are new to franchising some of the things in this book may not make any sense to you now, but when you re-read this after a while it will be crystal clear. So keep this book handy – you're going to need it as a reference.

I hope that for those of you that have been in franchising for awhile this book is a valuable tool to develop or retool your brand's strategic plan and helps you discover a few new nuggets of information or tools that you can implement immediately. If so, please let me know about it. I would like to hear how this book helped you out. You can email your comments directly to me at: lonnie@helgersonfranchisegroup.com.

What is a franchise Mega-Brand? And why is it so Important that your Franchise System be one?

While most people think of "mega" as something being very large, in this book it means something that is extraordinary and world class.

If you have read Jim Collins' book, *Good to Great* - this book translates to "Good is never good enough, but Mega is great and sustainable." In short, a Mega-Brand is a company that continuously excels to greatness. Throughout the book, I utilize franchise Mega-Brand "Best of Class" examples to illustrate the rules for successful franchising.

Use these rules in two important ways: as your guide to develop the corporate culture, habits, and best practices of franchise Mega-Brands and avoid the franchising Mega-Wrecks. Each chapter of this book starts with a franchising Mega-Wreck story and finishes at the end to illustrate the importance of each rule.

These are all true stories and some are quite dramatic so I chose not to reveal the brand name unless they are public companies or the story is already public.

Franchising has gone through all the economic cycles the rest of the world has experienced, but today, franchise companies continuously battle increased franchise regulation, legislative action, lack of financing, healthcare reform, and tighter location operating margins. With that said - there has never been a better time to start a franchised business.

The recession that started in 2008 has produced some tremendous opportunities and forged, or some cases *forced*, some franchise companies into what I classify as franchise Mega-Brands. This group is a blend of those that have been around for generations and those that are new, hundreds of units and those just starting.

If you are considering using franchising as an expansion and distribution method, or are already a franchise company you need to attract lenders for your franchisees, be sustainable and commit your entire organization's culture to becoming a competitive franchise Mega-Brand. This will help ensure your brand and franchisees are prepared to weather the next economic crisis.

Franchising today has become much like professional sports and you must approach it like you are heading to the Olympics. There may be room for a handful of players at the game, but only three of them will earn medals.

These rules should be your company's new strategic plan for competing in the Olympics® of franchising and it begins with Rule Numero Uno - franchisee profitability.

Rule No. 1 – Tee up your franchisees for mega-success, not failure!

In October 2004, I was listening intently to Meg Whitman, the then current CEO of eBay®, explain to conference attendees on how the Internet was fueling an unprecedented e-commerce growth.

Shortly after her presentation, my business partner and I met with her to discuss the feasibility of creating a retail franchise that would interface with eBay® to provide an auction item drop-off point direct to the customer. Since we were already management and shareholders of a respected growing technology franchise system, creating another franchise of eBay® drop-off stores to complement our existing brand seemed to make sense on the surface. What we were discussing with Meg Whitman was how to effectively reduce the transactional costs to make the contribution margin of each sale strong enough to create a profitable business model.

We were focused on trying to make sense of how a franchisee would make money at the store level. We had extensive experience in operating retail stores and knew what a franchisee's expenses would be, but the more we studied the costs of receiving, preparing and posting an item online, managing the listing, collecting the money, then paying the customer - there wasn't enough gross profit left at the end of the transaction to cover the overhead and make the business model work.

While we continued working on the concept's feasibility, scores of other eBay® drop-off franchises were opening up from coast-to-coast, with no sign of slow down. Were we missing something? Maybe... But first -

Why 5 Pennies Are Important To You!

I have served on the Board of Advisors for the International Institute for Franchise Executives (IIFE) at Nova Southeastern University in Ft. Lauderdale, FL for many years.

A fellow IIFE board member is Carolyn Bolton, Director of Special Projects for SUBWAY® Restaurants. Previously she was Brand Manager at Franchise Brands, LLC which was created in 2005 with the support and guidance of the founders of SUBWAY® Restaurants. Last year after a Nova Board meeting, Carolyn and I were chatting about how we are introducing our business experience to our kid's.

I shared with her that to teach my son Chandler some basic business skills I have him generate an invoice after cleaning my home office so I will pay him.

She told me that when she was still working with Franchise Brands, LLC her son Matthew, who was 8 or 9 at the time, would suggest to her that the company buy a doughnut chain or other concepts whose food he really liked.

Because of the frequency of his suggestions, she decided to teach him how they evaluate a franchise concept for acquisition – beginning with the store-level economics.

She told him that for every dollar (a hundred pennies) a store brings in a certain number of pennies must go to rent, others buy food for resale, some pay for insurance and labor, and so forth.

Finally, there must be room for five pennies (royalty) to go to the franchisor. She stressed that the payment of those five pennies must not compromise the ability of the franchisee to keep a good profit margin of pennies for themselves.

After Carolyn told me this story, I told her that I felt some franchise companies have forgotten about, or are not paying enough attention to those "5 Pennies" or franchisee profits these days.

We both agreed that it is an unfortunate fact that too many new franchisors quickly focus on how many locations they have, or how many stores they have sold rather than on the profits that a franchisee derives from them.

The bottom line: Without unit profits, there are no pennies available for a franchisor!

As an example, I remember standing in line waiting to get my badge at the International Franchise Association's 2007 annual convention in Las Vegas when I overheard two new franchisors talking about the big money they were going to make from their franchise fees. They had surmised that at $20K per franchise, if they sold only 10 locations they would have a nice $200,000 pot of money for themselves.

Before I could ask them if they thought that there might be more to franchising than getting rich off of large franchise fees, the staff waited on me, and when I turned

Franchise Mega-Brand's "Best of Class" at Franchisee Profitability

**7-Eleven®
(Over 42,000 Locations)**

Joseph M. DePinto, President & CEO

World's Largest Convenience Retailer

What started out as an ice house in Dallas, Texas, back in 1927 has grown and evolved into the world's largest operator, franchisor and licensor of convenience stores.

The company operates, franchises, and licenses approximately 7,600 stores in the U.S. and Canada. Of the more than 6,500 stores the company operates and franchises in the United States, more than 4,900 are franchised.

Outside of the U.S. and Canada, there are about 34,900 7-Eleven® and other convenience stores in Japan, Taiwan, Thailand, South Korea, China, Malaysia, Mexico, Singapore, Australia, Philippines, Indonesia, Norway, Sweden and Denmark.

around they were gone. As I walked away, I hoped that the convention would provide them an "awakening" to the reality and the seriousness of building a franchise system.

I have to wonder if since then they have gone out of business or have learned the importance of the "5 Pennies" and are still be operating.

How 5 Pennies can Make or Break a Franchise System

The hallmark of a franchise Mega-Brand is its intense attention to the unit economics of the system, or if you're new to franchising, the profitability of each individual operating store or unit.

The reality is that every system, no matter how large or well known, will have some locations that do not produce acceptable profits or perform at optimum levels. The key word here is "*some*", not "many", a "majority", or certainly not all of them.

There are simply too many variables involved with the operation of a franchised location not to have one or two low performers in a system. It may be in a poor location, unexpected construction takes place, bad management by the franchisee, not enough training, dirty restrooms, parking lot and facilities, bad tasting food or poor customer service. – the list goes on and on. The problems can spread throughout an entire system if not policed or intensely managed by the franchisor.

While these problems may initially appear small to deal with, they will wreak havoc on your brand equity through diminished sales and poor customer perception. Think about the last time that you stayed in a motel that was dirty, or ate in a restaurant that you had to wait forever to get your food. Have you gone back to them recently? Probably not.

Now imagine this problem happening to a franchise concept that struggles to make money, or doesn't fundamentally produce profits at all, and you have a recipe for disaster!

It is not only paramount that a concept makes enough money to cover the franchisors' *5 Pennies* and still produce a good profit for the franchisee, but the franchisor must continuously protect that store's profitability with a strong system.

Joe DePinto, CEO of 7-Eleven® (a best of class franchise Mega-Brand) refers to the depth of financial partnership with their franchisees as *"co-prosperity"* – meaning their franchisees are true financial partners in the brand.

The leaders of franchise Mega-Brands inherently understand the importance of franchisee profitability and focus the majority of their resources ensuring and growing it.

Franchising Fact: - If the 5 Pennies are not produced or guarded at the store level a franchise system is doomed for failure.

The Franchise Mega-Brand Model of Success

The Model of Success diagram (figure 1-1) illustrates the building blocks for growing a successful franchise Mega-Brand.

The strength of a pyramid is no stronger than its base. In this case franchisee profitability is the foundation upon which all aspects of the franchise model rely. If there are no franchisee profits the base erodes and crumbles causing the entire franchise system to collapse.

A strong Model of Success will couple franchisee profitability with an equally strong franchisor and team, building upon that foundation with layers of successful elements such as:

- Positive franchisee relations
- An ecosystem that promotes, develops, and shares system best practices

- A "good is never good enough" approach to training and support

- On-going development of programs to grow the system revenues

- Setting Key Performance Indicators, monitoring them system-wide as pro-active support and growth tools

- Growing the system methodically with the best franchisees possible

Figure 1-1 Franchise Mega-Brand Model of Success

As the strength of the system builds towards the top of the Model of Success, it continuously cascades tools, resources, programs, and efficiencies back to the base, creating additional franchisee profitability (figure 1-2) and refueling the entire model.

Figure 1-2 Franchise Mega-Brand Model of Success

Using the Model of Success example above, create one for your brand's strategic plan with initiatives, programs, and goals based upon the Ten Rules and tools contained in this book. This will bring alignment and focus to everyone on your team. Your team will understand your brand's strategic vision and the roadmap to getting there.

Author's Note: *Download a free editable Franchise Mega-Brand Model of Success template at www.FranchiseMegaBrand.com*

Developing a Culture of Financial Performance

Over the years I have heard countless potential franchisees tell me that they want to make a lot of money. Here is how a typical conversation about that subject goes,

Mr. Lonnie: *"So Mr. Candidate, can you define for me exactly what making a lot of money means?"*

Mr. Candidate: *"Well... I probably would like to make at least $100,000 per year."*

Mr. Lonnie: *"Great! Would that be gross revenue or net income?"*

Mr. Candidate: *"Ah... that would be net income."*

Mr. Lonnie: *"Excellent! So how much in gross revenues would you need to generate in order to produce $100,000 in net profit?"*

Mr. Candidate: *"Well... Uh..."* (followed by extended silence)

Hopefully you're smiling by now as this is exactly how these conversations go. The challenge and reality is that most prospective franchisees do not have a clue how to answer that question and relate to a business in the only way they can - which is comparing it to a job.

So here's the question – *How do you turn that conversation into an opportunity for you and your brand?*

Let's answer this for you by continuing the conversation,

Mr. Lonnie: *"That's OK Mr. Candidate, we don't expect you to have all the answers when it comes to our franchise. Let me help you out here. We have been in franchising for a long time and open a new Clippy Hippy hair salon about every six hours. Because of that, we know that for you to make the amount of money you just told me you would like to - will require the* *opening of three salons. Each of our hair salons average about $30-$40K per year in gross profits as reported by our franchisees and outlined in Item 19 of our Franchise Disclosure Document. That aligns exactly with your needs and expectations of income - doesn't it? "*

In this conversation I removed a common hurdle *"How much am I going to make?"* by educating the prospective franchisee on how our Clippy Hippy business model is viable investment and more than a paycheck.

Creating a culture of financial performance is not only important, it is a necessity. Periods of economic turmoil have made potential franchise candidates more cautious about a return on their investment.

It also sets the stage for two-way expectations:

1. (For the Potential Franchisee) It sets expectations of what they might expect to earn from a location and improves the franchise recruitment process.

2. (For the Franchisor) It defines the franchisor's expectations of the potential franchisees' financial performance.

To illustrate, let's continue the discussion with Mr. Candidate.

Mr. Lonnie: *"As you can see Mr. Candidate, we are serious about helping our franchisees realize their financial goals. It is ingrained in our system's culture. At the same time, we are seeking individuals that can generate the sales results necessary to achieve their goals, adhere to our process and methods, and help us develop brand domination in their market. Do you feel that you can meet those requirements, Mr. Candidate? "*

Developing a culture of financial performance such as this requires transparency from the franchisor and an Item 19 statement in the Franchise Disclosure Document (FDD). At the same time it sets a benchmark of expectation for both the franchisee and the franchisor.

There are a couple of key things we learned in franchising during the last few years - that transparency and partnership concerning Return on Investment (ROI) has become an absolute expectation of candidates.

Item 19 Financial Performance Representations (FPR)

I have been a fan of an Item 19 FPR since I started my career with Super 8 Motels® over 25 years ago and the reasons are simple:

- It answered the question about how much revenue a franchisee could expect to produce with a motel
- It provided benchmarking data to us at headquarters
- It sold more franchises.

An Item 19 FPR in your FDD can include written, oral, or visual financial references that allow a prospective franchise owner to determine probable, stated, or an estimated financial range of gross sales, gross or net profits, income, cost of goods, or other operational metrics.

Back in the 80's Super 8 Motels'® Item 19 statement included the Average Daily Rate (ADR), Average Occupancy Percentage, and percentage of reservations provided by the national reservation center. From those numbers a franchisee candidate could quickly determine what a property could potentially produce in revenue.

No. of Rooms x (Average Occupancy %) x ADR = Revenue per Day

x 365 = Forecasted Annual Revenue

Can I include GGS' P/L?

Today – Super 8 Motels® provides a more elaborate FPR in Item 19 than this example, but the point is that this basic formula helped grow the chain with hundreds and hundreds of new properties on an annual basis.

Even though your system may be very new and with few operating units, there is probably some data or metrics (such as above) that can provide a fundamental understanding of your unit economics to a potential franchisee. If you had profitable operating units prior to franchising (as outlined and required in Rule No. 10), the financial results from those locations may be utilized for an Item 19.

A franchisor is not required to include an FPR in Item 19, and there are specific reasons why you may choose not to include one, but today it is estimated that over 40% of franchise brands include one, and that percentage continues to grow. If your system has an investment level that requires periodic financing, to even be considered in today's lending climate you absolutely need to have an Item 19 for lenders to review.

Remember, if you do not have an FPR in your FDD, no one in your organization can discuss any financial performance expectations with franchise candidates.

> *Franchise Mega-Brand's "Best of Class" at Franchisee Profitability*
>
> **Service Brands International**
>
> **Molly Maid®**
> **Mr. Handyman®**
> **ProTect Painters®**
> **1-800 DryClean®**
>
> **David McKinnon, CEO**
>
> Service Brands International is a privately held, multi-concept franchise system with worldwide headquarters in Ann Arbor, Michigan.
>
> Since 1984, SBI has honed their skills, designed innovative operating systems, and meticulously burnished their reputation as an essential service provider in the marketplace and as a bellwether company within the franchising industry.

Franchise Mega-Brands know that a compelling FPR makes a powerful tool in recruiting new franchisees into their franchise systems. I agree and strongly recommend using them.

Author's Note: *Please consult with your franchise attorney concerning any and all legal questions relating to Item 19 and Franchise Disclosure Documents.*

Assisting Profitability through Alternative Financing

Back in the old days of at least four or five years ago most franchisors didn't get involved with franchise financing. The economic downturn and subsequent lack of credit access changed that game. Today, a franchise brand must be involved with finance and lending at every level or it will not grow. There is no choice.

During the last few years of economic turmoil, franchisors who had established lending relationships were able to continue getting deals financed, although fewer of them. Finance tools that rose to the top during the last few years were the SBA Franchise Registry and the Bank Credit Report. These tools help franchisees attain financing to either build out new locations or refinance existing debt loads by educating lenders about the brand and gaining their support.

The Bank Credit Report is a relatively new tool developed by Darrell Johnson of FRANdata to provide lenders an objective credit department style (underwriting) analysis of a franchise brand's financial and operation risks, franchise system and unit performance risks written in "banker language". For franchisors this means the franchisees' loan process is streamlined.

The Small Business Administration (SBA) Franchise Registry is a list of franchise companies that have been reviewed and approved by the SBA for lending, helping to expedite the loan process for SBA-backed loans.

How do we get on the SBA Fran. Registry?

We all know that the days of carefree, easy lending are gone. That means for a franchise to remain competitive a franchisor must be directly involved and actively engaging finance alternatives for their system. These tools help you accomplish that.

Author's Note: *For more information on both of these programs visit www.FranchiseMegaBrand.com or www.FRANdata.com*

Franchisor Financial Assistance Programs

Nothing speaks louder about a franchisor's commitment to franchisee success and profitability than a franchisor participating in the startup phase of a new location by establishing cost controls.

In reaction to the most recent economic meltdown some franchisors began to waive royalty fees for periods of time, discount their franchise fees, enact discounted purchasing requirements, and create other cost controlling measures for franchisees.

While some brands offered these breaks temporarily to ease the effects of the downturn, other brands adopted these measures and incentives on a more permanent basis to effectively grow their system. Some created interesting partner programs such as Service Brands International's (SBI) money-back guarantee. SBI is the parent company of Molly Maid®, ProTect Painters®, and Mr. Handyman® and offers a full refund of the franchise fee if the franchisee does not attain $150,000 in gross sales within 18 months of operation. At the time of this writing, the SBI money-back guarantee was a temporary offering, but is being considered as a permanent program.

Regardless, this offer conveys the confidence that SBI, as a franchise Mega-Brand, has in their business models. All other brands should strive to emulate this level of confidence.

A review of the hard costs associated with opening and supporting a new franchise location until its royalty stream covers those costs will give you insight to the options and incentives that you can offer. Doing this yields significant returns in positive franchisee relations.

Franchisee Unit Profitability Tools Guide

Tool	What it Does	Rule
KPI's & metrics.	Proactive monitoring of units' KPI's through Point of Sale (POS) & Franchise Information Systems will provide advanced notice of those franchisees that are struggling or those drifting off course.	No. 9 - Manage your system like NASA would.
Franchisee Performance Groups	A group of 6-8 franchise owners that meet on a regular basis and deep-dive into financial, operational, planning, and marketing best practices.	No. 5 – Plant, cultivate, and harvest system best practices.
Expense Reduction	Management of franchisees' costs of on-going supplies, real estate, operational expenses and purchases. Expense reduction should be done for each line item in your system's Standard Chart of Accounts.	No. 7 - Focus on where the rubber hits the racetrack.
Sharing Best Practices	Provides best practices cultivated from the entire franchise system to increase unit-level profitability.	No. 5 – Plant, cultivate, and harvest system best practices.
Alternative Financing Resources	Partnering with multiple lending sources provides alternatives for franchisees to restructure current loan packages and/or gain additional expansion capital. *How to do this?*	No. 1 - Tee up your franchisees for mega-success, not failure!

30

National Accounts	Creating and administering a National Accounts Program drives additional revenues directly to franchise units, with little or no customer acquisition cost.	No. 8 - Create partners in growth.
Franchisor Financial Assistance Programs	Provides relief for royalties, advertising fees, and/or other fees during their new business startup period through discounts or waivers. _what are these?_	No. 1 - Tee up your franchisees for mega-success, not failure!
National/ Regional Marketing & Advertising Programs	Uses funds contributed by all franchisees to actively promote and drive sales to franchised locations either nationally or regionally. _local websites_	No. 7 - Focus on where the rubber hits the racetrack.
FDD Item 19 Financial Performance Representation	Provides data and metrics to help potential franchisees determine the financial viability and profitability potential of a franchised location.	No. 1 - Tee up your franchisees for mega-success, not failure!
Bank Credit Report _Where do I get this?_	Provides the franchisee's banker understandable underwriting information not easily discerned through the FDD and therefore streamlines the loan process.	No. 1 - Tee up your franchisees for mega-success, not failure!
Underperforming Unit Response Team	A team of subject matter experts that specialize in assisting distressed franchised locations.	No. 7 - Focus on where the rubber hits the racetrack.

Rule Summary

Nothing is more important than a franchisee's ability to generate profits. Without it you, as a franchisor, have no reason to be in existence. And if so – it won't be for long.

Throughout my career, I have often told my franchisees that I wish for them to own a new Mercedes®, a big house, and their own jet. If they achieved that - I knew the automatic by-product would be the incredibly wild success enjoyed by us as their franchisor!

The Franchise Mega-Brand Model of Success, tools, and programs outlined throughout this book will assist you to create a strategic plan that preserves franchisee profitability and protects the 5 Pennies that are critical to your brand's market dominance.

Key Points

- The success of your system is dependent on sustainable and strong unit economics.

- Protect the unit economics and the 5 Pennies.

- Build a franchise Mega-Brand Model of Success for your brand.

- Develop a culture of financial performance by using tools such as an FPR, bank credit reports, and the SBA Franchise Registry.

- Help your owners succeed by financially participating with them.

Franchise Mega-Brand's "Best of Quotes" on Franchisee Profitability

"Franchisee profitability is the most important mission of the franchisor!"

– Fred DeLuca, President and Co-Founder, SUBWAY® Restaurants

Continued from the beginning of the chapter:

My partners and I had concluded that we could not develop a profitable eBay® store model and decided to drop our plans.

Within a few short years of hyper growth, eBay® stores had shown up everywhere across the United State, and just as quickly as they opened, they began to close.

Unfortunately for hundreds and hundreds of trusting franchisees that invested into the eBay® store concepts, the stores were unprofitable and subsequently closed their doors. This is - *A franchising Mega-Wreck!*

Rule No. 2 – Franchising is a mega-relationship business!

A few years ago, the CEO of an established restaurant chain asked me to assist him with some challenges his franchise system was facing. We had gotten to know each other through some meetings and from what I knew he seemed to have a successful brand. His concept was Caribbean-themed, sit-down restaurants which had been in business for many, many years. He had started expanding the chain through franchising and, at the time, his system had about 28 locations, of which 6 or 8 were corporately owned.

It didn't take me more than one meeting at his office to figure out what was ailing the system – it was him and his negative attitude towards his franchisees!

He was extremely combative with his franchisees because he did not understand franchise relations or the general principals of being a franchisor. The overall situation was so bad that there were several lawsuits against him which were devouring large amounts of his and the franchisees' cash.

My advice to him was straightforward. He had two choices: Sell his corporate restaurants and focus on franchising by hiring someone with strong franchise experience to run the company, settle the lawsuits, and restore the franchisee relationships, or sell the franchise operations to someone and then continue as a franchisee of the new system.

If he didn't make a decision soon, the enormous cost of the legal battles would end up taking the entire system down, including the corporate locations. I warned him that he didn't have much time, and for the sake of the system that he make a decision quickly.

At the end of the chapter, find out which direction he went...

You Have Two Distinct Relationships with a Franchisee

Franchise Mega-Brand leaders recognize that their systems operate on two very different but equally important relationship levels with their franchise owners. First is the <u>legal</u> relationship between the franchisor and franchisee that is defined in the Franchise Agreement. The second one is the <u>operating</u> relationship *most important* between the franchisor and the franchisee - which is communicated through company culture and philosophy.

Of these two, the operating relationship is the most important because it will lead to fewer negative, legal relationships in the long run.

I often tell people that the best franchisee relationship lesson I ever had was becoming a parent to my four children. It's not because franchisees act like children, but because I learned how to respond when questions are asked or comments are made.

Franchise Mega-Brand's "Best of Class" at Franchisee Relations

A&W®
Long John Silver's®

Sid Feltenstein

In 1995, Sid led a private equity investment group that acquired A&W® Restaurants. Under his leadership, the chain grew from 450 to almost 1,000 units in just five years.

In 1999, Sid led A&W's® purchase of Long John Silver's®. Under his leadership, A&W®/Long John Silver's® sales grew five times and its operating profits grew by 40 times.

The company was sold to YUM!® Brands in 2002 in a highly successful transaction - primarily from Sid's exceptional leadership and his ability to foster strong relations with his franchisees.

My kids taught me how to be patient, and most importantly, <u>to ask clarifying questions frequently</u> until I know exactly what they are trying to communicate.

I take the same patient, inquisitive approach to franchisee communication and use it as an opportunity for system improvement and/or franchisee education.

In many instances, I (as the franchisor) learned a lot from the franchisees and improved the systems.

The Relationship Opportunity

At one of the International Franchise Association's annual conventions I attended a break-out session that was geared towards franchisee relations. One of the panelists was Sid Feltenstein (who is highlighted in this chapter).

At that time, Sid had acquired A&W® and Long John Silver's®, which he turned around and then sold to Yum!® Brands. The A&W® and Long John Silver's® turnaround was, and still is, a very successful story in franchising.

Sid was asked what the *"secret"* to the successful turnaround of the company was. Sid's reply was simple and one that I have never forgotten. He said, *"I asked the franchisees what needed to be fixed and provided it for them."* In other words, he saw opportunity to engage the franchisees in the process, value their opinion, and then leverage that relationship to enhance and induce change into the brands.

Of course, not all of us are dealing with change at this magnitude, however, even normal, day-to-day, incremental change requires positive and *"engaging"* relationships to ensure alignment of goals between you and your franchisees to clear up any misperceptions in communications.

Not a Free-for-All

Fostering positive franchisee relations does not mean that you create a free-for-all or a democracy in your system. It simply means that you create engaging ways for franchisees to be involved in the direction of the system and that you're willing to listen to them.

When franchisees are directly involved and valued they can become apostles and advocates for you and that can quickly build system-wide communication.

Because franchisees tend to listen to other franchisees with less skepticism than they might their franchisor, having franchisee "buy-in" always aids better system communications and relations.

And the more buy-in the better!

Aren't Relationships a Reason People Join a Franchise System?

Think about this for a minute: People are drawn to franchising because they want to be a part of something much larger and supportive and not operating their business alone. In fact we as franchisors capitalize on this emotional draw everyday!

The statement, *"In business for yourself - but not by yourself"* has almost become a cliché used repeatedly in franchise recruiting presentations.

But is the strength of that statement always applied within the system in the same manner that it comes across in the recruiting process?

During the franchise recruiting process franchisors inundate prospective franchisees with messaging about the opportunity, interviews, discovery day, phone calls, etc. This creates an incredibly high-touch culture.

At no time in the lifecycle of a franchise are the franchisees more excited than after the initial courtship when they are getting ready to open their shiny new business.

Some owners may feel alienated, let down or even have buyer's remorse if that high-touch level of support from the franchisor is not continued after the sale. Whether or not a franchisee shares these feelings will depend upon their personality, but rest assured they may be there, and if not addressed in some fashion, may create problems in the future.

Franchise Mega-Brand leaders develop a culture that grows the franchisee relationship on all levels knowing that if they lack consistent positive relationships with the franchisees it will cause them to miss the signs of a trouble.

Developing a Culture of Engagement Begins at the Top!

Tom Feltenstein and Mac Anderson wrote a great little book called *Change is Good... You Go First.* I have always loved that title because those six little words really put the difficulty of change into perspective.

In the chapter called *"Let Your Actions Speak"* is this quote:

> *To change any culture, in any company, the people at the top have to show it! Because words without deeds mean nothing!*

How do your actions stack up against this quote?

The Ten Question Relationship Test

Here are ten important questions to ask yourself and your teams that will help you assess your current culture and actions towards franchisee relations:

1. *What are we doing to continue and ensure a high-touch experience with the franchisees in our system?*

2. Do we manage the system with any transparency?

3. How would our franchisees rate our engagement with them?

4. How do we react to franchisees when new ideas are brought forth for consideration?

5. Does our corporate culture really "walk the talk" that our brand information promises in the recruiting process? Are we all directly involved with the process?

6. Do our franchisees perceive us as honest and trustworthy?

7. Do we actively seek input from our franchisees ?

8. Does anyone on our staff show favoritism or practice retribution toward any franchisee? How is it policed?

9. Would our franchisees say that we genuinely care about their input on the direction of the system?

10. Do we tend to rely on the legal relationship before we try to work issues out through the operating relationship with our franchisees?

Developing a culture of great franchisee engagement and relations doesn't happen overnight. It takes time, consistent championing by leadership, a ton of hard work, and a commitment to constant system improvement.

Some Tools to Improve Franchisee Relations

Fostering great franchisee relations requires both <u>engagement</u> and <u>communications</u> within the system. The following two tables list programs and tools that can be used to improve both of these areas.

Franchisee "System Engagement" Programs

Franchisee Involvement	What it Does
Franchisee Advisory Council (FAC)	Provides a means for the franchisees and the

	franchisor to discuss topics that are relevant to the system as a whole respecting the input of each.
Marketing/Advertising Advisory Council (MAC)	Used primarily as a management or advisory committee for National and/or Regional Marketing and Advertising funds.
Strategic Planning	Provides for the direct or indirect involvement of franchisees in the company's annual strategic planning process.
Training	Involves qualified franchisees in the training of new franchisees and/or on-going training of existing owners.
Special Interest/Focus Groups	Franchisee groups that are assembled for specific projects or technology needs.
Best Practices Group	Franchisee group that focuses on the cultivation and assessment of best practices in the system, which could include operations, marketing, real estate, and business management practices.
Mentoring	A program that matches successful franchisees with others to mentor and coach to excel or overcome obstacles.
Conference/Convention Planning	A group that assesses and provides guidance and for conventions and conferences.
User Groups	Franchisee and staff groups that provide input on specific areas. (i.e. technology and point of sale systems (POS))
Purchasing Cooperatives	Franchisees that collectively purchase products at preferred rates. Can also serve in an advisory capacity.
Grass Roots Government Relations	Encourages franchisees to get involved with local, state, and federal issues that affect small business and franchising.

Franchisee "Communication" Tools

Method of Communication	What it Does
Surveys and Polls	Used to solicit feedback from the entire system on a variety of issues and topics including an annual franchisor score card.
CEO System Calls	A regularly scheduled call or webinar to update the system or showcase franchisee best practices.
Field Representatives and Franchisee Support Coaches	The frontline representative of the franchisor that provides support and communications directly to franchises.
Franchisee Intranet or Extranet	An electronic system used for company news, newsletters, discussion forums, email, document storage and a host of other communication tools.
Regional Meetings	Geo-targeted meetings between franchisor and franchisee to solicit communications and feedback.
Social Networking	Uses Twitter, Facebook, LinkedIn, YouTube, and other social networking sites to communicate with franchisees.
Phone Calls	The most overlooked and easiest way to improve franchisee communications.
E-mail	An effective tool for communication, but has the highest probability of misinterpretation.
Annual Convention	Systemwide gathering of all franchisees for networking, education, and communications.
Operations Manuals	Unit operations guidelines and communications.

Author's Note: *The IFA's Franchise Relations Committee has produced a handbook called "Improved Communications Means Improved Franchise Relations" that provides a more detailed list of electronic, print, and channel- specific franchisee* *communication tools. The handbook is available for electronic download at* www.FranchiseMegaBrand.com

Does this Mean I Have to Learn How to Learn How to Sing Kumbaya?

Definitely not, but it does mean you need to learn how to balance and weigh the input from franchisees against the goals of franchise management.

Franchisees should not and do not want to run the franchise system. What they do want is to run their locations knowing that their voice has been heard and that the franchisor is respectful when making decisions affecting them.

A Healthy System Needs a Little Friction to Stay Relevant

A franchise system with no franchisee/franchisor disagreements at any level is stagnating and ripe for a competitor to enter, take the advantage and dominate the space!

Healthy disagreements, handled the right way, can lead to system improvement. That improvement, when promoted by the franchisor can lead to growth and opportunity. Many disagreements are based on misaligned perceptions and views. Both the franchisees and the franchisor are working to reach the same success but are taking entirely different roads to get there.

The franchisor is traveling on the brand-based, macro-view road, while the franchisee is diligently traveling on the location-based, micro-view road.

To illustrate this, here is a true story. A franchisee of mine called me one day and told me he had the definitive answer for increased sales – giving his customers locally-made candy.

After telling him how happy I was to hear his sales were increasing, I asked him if he had benchmarked and measured the results before and after he started the initiative.

He said he had not, but just *knew* it was working because all his customers were telling him how much they loved the candy. I explained that in order to roll out a new program to the entire system we needed thorough testing for quantified results.

At this point, he began to get irritated with me because he felt that I didn't care about his idea. I told him I cared deeply about his idea, but the fact was that people's tastes vary around the country and what is a popular item in his area may not be in other franchisee's territory.

When he heard this he immediately understood my point and agreed with me. He admitted that he hadn't considered that and felt somewhat embarrassed. I asked him if he knew how the McDonald's® Big Mac®, Ronald McDonald® character, and the Fillet-O-Fish came to be, to which he replied, "no."

I explained to him that all of these famous items were franchisee inventions and that franchisees should never hesitate to call with an idea because it might be a winner!

Before this we were acquaintances, but because of this call we became good friends and developed a great relationship that still lasts.

From this true example it is clear that the franchisee was focused on the location-based micro view and the perceived increase of sales from the candy. His personal measurement was purely anecdotal. Mine was the brand-based, macro view which was about measurement and quantifying its affect on the entire system.

This conversation could have easily had different results had I not taken the time to explain and educate the franchisee on my perspective and how the process works for a system. This is proof that a little communication goes a long, long way.

What Happens When Relations Turn Sour?

It's inevitable that sooner or later you will run into disagreement with someone over something regardless of how well your intentions or how good the relationships are.

The route you take to resolve your differences will depend on the severity of the issue and how far apart the parties are concerning an agreement. Disagreements can be as simple as my candy example or as complex as a number of franchisees banding together to fight costing factors, system direction or other serious challenges.

If a personal phone call doesn't resolve the issue try sitting down with the franchisee and talking about the issue. My personal approach is, *"Let's not let the cost of an airline ticket get in the way of patching things up."* After all, a day or two out of the office and the cost of travel are a whole lot cheaper than the cost of litigation.

There are also many benefits to a face-to-face meeting at a franchisees' location:

1. It makes the statement, "You care enough about the franchisee to travel to the location."

2. It helps minimize the drama of the disagreement by quickly addressing it firsthand.

3. It promotes good faith efforts to resolve on behalf of the franchisor should the disagreement escalate further.

If face-to-face meetings and other attempts do not bring resolution, then Alternative Dispute Resolution must be pursued.

Mediation and Arbitration for Dispute Resolution

Two Alternative Dispute Resolution tools that many franchisors have written into their Franchise Agreements are mediation and arbitration.

Mediation uses a third-party, trained mediator who works as a go-between to the parties and assists them in reaching an agreement. The benefit to mediation is that it is a much less expensive alternative to court for both parties and it introduces a knowledgeable third party into the negotiations.

At the beginning of the mediation process both parties work to choose a mediator who often has previous franchise experience. I find a skilled mediator with franchise experience can bring agreement quicker by providing an "outsider's franchise education" to both parties.

The downside to mediation is that it is non-binding, neither the mediator nor a judge hands down a ruling that both parties are required to adhere to.

If the disagreement is not resolved through mediation or the dispute requires a ruling between the parties then arbitration is an alternative. Unlike mediation, arbitration results in a binding decision imposed upon the parties by the arbitrator and are enforceable in court.

Both mediation and arbitration are excellent alternative dispute resolution tools and ones that I highly recommend using should the need arise.

Author's Note: Don't wait for a crisis to happen to learn about dispute resolution! Consult with your franchise attorney to learn about and fully understand the legal methods of dispute resolution and how to best integrate them into your franchise system.

Strengthening Relations through Brand Standards Compliance

Franchisees buy in and fully expect that their franchisor is ensuring brand standards and consistency throughout the franchise system. When brand standards are not monitored and enforced by the franchisor the "goodwill value" of a franchisee's business is eroded, and so is the franchisee's respect and trust for the franchisor. Over time this neglect will have an adverse affect on the goodwill value of the *entire* system and will ultimately lead to diminished relations with franchisees.

Because of this it is imperative that a brand standards compliance program be implemented from day one. Policing brand compliance can be difficult for new and emerging franchisors because they are afraid of the effect on the royalty stream if locations close and the negative perception of potential new franchisees.

As tough as this may seem, standards must be policed to ensure the long-term health and viability of a franchise system.

Trust me on this one. You will gain much more respect, credibility, and system buy-in from potential new franchisees by telling them that you closed locations because you wouldn't compromise your standards than you would by letting those locations continue to break the rules.

During my tenure as CEO of Ident-A-Kid®, I initiated newer and tougher brand-standards compliance programs which ultimately led to losing a few locations because they would not comply with them.

It was only later, when I had *many* franchise owners thank me for setting the bar higher, that I discovered how deeply franchise relations tied to compliance. They appreciated me dealing with the non-conformers of the system and improving the value of their franchised business.

Did this have an effect on our franchise recruiting efforts? Absolutely! However, it was positive because it improved our franchisees' validation of the strength of the brand and that we were willing to protect it.

Rule Summary

Great franchisee relations are like strong stitches that hold the fabric of a franchise brand together. If the relations start to weaken or come unraveled the entire system begins to fall apart and crumble.

Creating great franchisee relationships is not all that difficult, but it does require commitment, honesty, and transparency. There are no secrets in your franchise system because every system has the "underground" franchisee grapevine that reports your every move. The more transparency you create the less need for the grapevine to exist.

Key Points

- *Remember that you have two different relationships with franchisees.*
- *Make relationship building an opportunity to improve the system.*
- *Developing a positive franchise relations culture begins at the top.*
- *Take the ten question relationship test.*
- *Use system engagement and communication tools to foster positive relationships.*
- *Remember, sometimes "heads have to roll" when things get out of hand.*
- *Build and enforce healthy system compliance standards.*

Franchise Mega-Brand's "Best of Quotes" on Franchisee Relations

"There is no 'I' in Wendy's® - The first two letters are 'WE'."

– Dave Thomas, Founder, Wendy's® International, Inc. 1932-2002

At some point in our lives we have all been told to treat others as you would like to be treated. This is the rule you have to live by to build a franchise Mega-Brand.

Continued from the beginning of the chapter:

Remember the guy who was in a quagmire of lawsuits with his franchisees because of his inability to listen or get along with his franchisees? Unfortunately, he decided to leave things as they were and soon thereafter the entire restaurant system went into bankruptcy and closed their doors. *A franchising Mega-Wreck!*

Rule No. 3 – Franchising is not a drag race it is more like the 24 hours of Daytona.

I attended a franchise conference in Ft. Lauderdale where I met a couple of guys that were brand new franchisors. As we talked they were telling me how they were growing fast by selling large Area Representative Agreements requiring each Area Representative to sell and open many franchisees stores.

They were selling so many of these contracts because their single-unit franchisees did quite well financially. This was due to the strong support and training they provided. However, they were starting to run into huge challenges with their Area Representatives. They were unable to meet their development schedules and were not opening enough stores and didn't really know how to get them back on track.

In other words, they were selling lots of store opening commitments but not getting them open with single-unit operators.

So I said, *"It sounds like you really know how to open and support single stores and make them profitable. But who on your staff directly supports your Area Representatives and holds them accountable for their territories' success?"*

They both gave me a blank stare and a long pause of silence.

At the end of the chapter, find out what caused these guys to hold their breath and what has happened with their system since then.

The Lure of Rapid Franchise Growth

Every franchisor (including me) wants to be the next McDonald's® or SUBWAY® Restaurants. In countless pieces of franchise opportunity literature I read, *"Our goal is..."* or *"We are set to be..."* or *"We are the McDonald's® of the (you insert the sector)."*

The reality of course is that out of the thousands of franchise systems that exist, very few ever grow beyond a couple hundred locations.

Yet there are those seemingly unknown systems that seem to spring up overnight and achieve fame such as Five Guy's®, Massage Envy®, and Liberty Tax Service®.

So how did they do it?

Faster System Expansion Strategies

In addition to selling single unit franchises, all of these companies grew exponentially by using some variation of larger territory/multiple unit sales strategies to grow.

Multi-Unit Growth Strategies

Type	Description
Area Development Franchises	An Area Development franchise is much like a single unit franchise, but the franchisee is granted the right to open multiple locations on a predetermined schedule in a larger, defined, geographic area.
Area Representative Franchises	Area Representatives (sometimes referred to as **Regional Developer**) are typically granted a larger geographic area and generally take on the responsibility of recruiting and supporting individual franchisees within that area. In return, the Area Representative typically shares in the upfront initial franchise fee and ongoing royalties.
Master Franchise (Sub-Franchise) Agreements	The Master Franchisee is granted the rights to sub-franchise a concept in a specific geographic territory, state or country. In essence a Master Franchisee becomes a "mini" franchisor for that territory. Typically, Master Franchise agreements are utilizing for International franchise expansion.

The two most common franchise development strategies used domestically are Area Development and Area Representative.

Is a Multi-Unit Growth Strategy Right for Every Franchise System?

Not necessarily. It depends upon a number of factors including the franchised unit operations, age of the system, geographic footprint already in place, and internal support structures.

Many service franchise brands require owner/operators because their economic models are not conducive to multi-unit expansion.

Part of the strategic planning for a franchise system should include evaluating multi-unit growth and the correct approach to it.

However, if a franchise system has been operating for a longer period of time and wants to provide a scalable growth plan for existing franchise owners, then a structured Area Development plan may make sense.

Again, the answer to the question is not a simple one.

Because each franchise system is very different the decision will be difficult and needs to be thought

Franchise Mega-Brand's "Best of Class" at Sustained High Growth

SUBWAY® Restaurants (Over 36,000 Locations)

Fred DeLuca President and Co-Founder

Back in 1965, Fred DeLuca set out to fulfill his dream of becoming a medical doctor. Searching for a way to help pay for his education, a family friend suggested he open a submarine sandwich shop. With a loan of $1,000, the friend, Dr. Peter Buck, offered to become Fred's partner, and a business relationship that would change the landscape of the fast food industry was forged.
Today, the SUBWAY® brand is the world's largest submarine sandwich chain with more than 36,000 locations around the world.
From the beginning, Fred has had a clear vision for the future of the SUBWAY® brand.

through carefully.

Both of these multi-unit strategies can grow a franchise system dramatically if the program is well executed with the right Area Development or Area Representative candidates/owners.

On the other hand, if you have the wrong people in place, or do not provide them with the level of support required to execute at this level, the consequences can be devastating.

The Advantages

In addition to the accelerated franchise growth these development strategies can provide, there are a number of other direct benefits:

- Increased sales revenues from selling larger territories and multiple-location commitments
- Territory-franchisee profitability should be increased by having a responsible and accountable party for it
- Direct-franchisee field support can be provided by Area Developers and Representatives
- Increased geographic-specific marketing and advertising can be accomplished through collective franchisee co-ops
- Strong local knowledge is provided by the Area Developers and Representatives
- Provides for a quicker response to real estate opportunities
- Fosters better franchisee relationships and communications
- Provides alignment and focus on targeted market growth and brand penetration.

The Disadvantages

While the benefits of these types of growth strategies can be very compelling, there are dangers that can create disasters for a franchise system.

- Having an Area Developer or Representative that does not:
    - Provide the level of support required
    - Communicate with or treat franchisees well
    - Meet location sales and opening requirements
    - Represent the brand well or is a poor operator
    - Adhere to the franchisor's prescribed methods of doing business.
- Area Development and Representative Agreements are typically long term and may lock the franchisor out the territory
- May create different geographic pockets of brand culture
- In the event that the parent franchise company is sold and Area Developers or Representatives disagree with sale transaction, the possibility of pushback exists.
- The sharing of fees and the effect of the decreased revenues on the franchisor.

Successful Strategic Market Buildout

In the early 90's, shortly after I started Computer Doctor® (my first chain), I met and became friends with Ray Barton the Chairman of Great Clips®.

One day, while visiting him at his headquarters in Minneapolis, MN Ray asked me how many Computer Doctor® stores I was planning on building in the Minneapolis/St. Paul market.

Without hesitation I told him 24 locations, one in every suburb. He smiled and told me that is exactly how many Great Clips® had initially planned to open there as well.

He then asked me how many salons I thought they currently had in the market, to which I guessed at around 50-75. He said that was a good guess, but they actually have 120 or so and still growing. He then gave me some advice that I have never forgotten.

"Lonnie," he said, *"What you know today about your unit operations will change in two years, five years, and certainly ten or twenty years. Never give too much territory away, as the geography required to generate that location's sales will change. Always measure that and make adjustments as you grow."*

"Because of that, we open a new territory only when we are ready to pour the resources into it that are required to be successful. We thoroughly build out the market and then move on to another."

What Great Clips®, as a franchise Mega-Brand, has done exceedingly well is concentric market development. They started with a supportable market and grew out in concentric circles until the market was completely developed.

Franchise Mega-Brand's "Best of Class" at Strategic Market Buildout

Great Clips®

**Ray Barton, Chairman of the Board
Rhoda Olsen, CEO**

Since 1983, Great Clips® has grown from four salons with annual sales of less than $1 million in 1983 to more than 3,000 salons in more than 140 markets with annual sales of more than $850 million in 2009. A key to Great Clips'® success is its dedication to the franchisees' success. Great Clips® grows because its franchisees are successful and profitable. Great Clips® focuses on providing franchisees with excellent training, services and support, based on the understanding that customers have choices—the brand that can best give customers what they want will become the biggest and most successful.

Concentric market development is franchising 101, yet is the hardest strategy for new and emerging franchisors to stick with because of what I call the *"Urgency to grow and can't say no!"* syndrome, or in other words – the need to make a sale because of a shortage of cash. (Refer to Rule No. 10 for more on this topic.)

Great Clips® has never wavered on its commitment to concentric market development and the size and strength of their system is testament to this brand-growth strategy.

Ten Keys to a Successful Area Developer or Representative Program

1. *Recruiting the right qualified candidate as an Area Developer or Representative*

2. *Providing dedicated support and coaching to them*

3. *Jointly developing localized marketing and networking plans for recruiting new single unit franchisees in the territory*

4. *Establishing a realistic territory size and development schedule that can be met*

5. *Integrating them into your corporate infrastructure*

6. *Hosting required quarterly Area Developer or Representative only meetings*

7. *Setting realistic territory unit sales goals, single unit development goals and holding them accountable for it*

8. *Provide them with dashboard and metrics tools to effectively manage their territory*

9. *Poll their territory franchisees to grade the Area Developer or Representative on their franchisee relationships, support and other operational items*

10. *Providing specialized and advanced operations training to them.*

Rule Summary

While Area Development or Area Representation may not be suitable for every franchise system, Darryl Johnson, CEO of FRANdata, indicates that over 50% of franchised systems today have multi-unit owners and this trend continues to grow.

It is important to remember the title of this rule and that building a successful franchise is a race of endurance, not speed. Fast-track growth without proper planning or execution will cause significant problems that may or may not be able to be resolved. For that reason, learn from the success of franchise Mega-Brands such as SUBWAY® Restaurants and Great Clips® that grew strategically and through concentric market development.

Beware of the *"Urgency to grow and can't say no!"* syndrome and your system will be much, much stronger in the long run.

Key Points

- *Determine if multi-unit growth makes sense for your brand.*

- *Focus on concentric growth if applicable.*

- *Remember the ten keys to successful multi-unit franchising.*

- *Grow methodically, because growing too fast is not a good thing!*

Continued from the beginning of the chapter:

We began this chapter with a story about a discussion I had with a couple of newer franchisors and their challenges with their Area Representatives.

After their long dramatic pause after my question they indicated this was somewhat of an epiphany for them. It was most likely what was wrong with their system because they didn't have any sales or operations support for their Area Representatives. As they grew, they built training and support for their stores, not realizing that Area Representatives also need support, albeit a different type and level of support.

I went on to explain to them that at the stage of life their system is at, the least expensive part of the lesson for them will be implementing support and training for their Area Representatives.

The real challenge is that some of their current Area Representatives may not be the right people for the job, meaning they will need to figure out a way to get them growing or exit the system.

In addition to that, most if not all, of the Area Representatives were behind on their development schedule. Because of this, they will need to either get them current with their obligations or re-evaluate the existing development schedules and file extensions for them to meet the schedule. The worst case scenario is to terminate them.

No matter how you slice it, fixing the problem will take their eye off the goal, devour some cash and set them back for an extended period of time. The lesson learned here is that you can quickly outstrip resources and support mechanisms in your franchise system if you grow too fast.

Bottom line: High sales growth does not equal success. - *A franchising Mega-Wreck!*

Rule No. 4 – Do not have an accountant remove a brain tumor!

Franchising is *"a business of being in business"* and it requires franchise-specific management skills and expertise to be successful at it.

Many years ago I received a call from a gentleman who, at the time, had purchased a competing franchise chain to the one that I owned, and was wondering if I might be able to help him.

I replied, *"Absolutely!"* and he began to explain that for many years before he bought the franchise system he had been a senior executive for a national grocery chain. To diversify, he had purchased a couple of franchise locations as an investment. The stores performed so well that he decided to buy the entire franchise system.

He continued to tell me that he was trying to get his franchisees to run their stores *exactly* like his corporate locations but they were not listening or doing what he told them to do. I told him, *"Of course not. They are franchisees, not employees. But if you demonstrate and coach them long enough with quantifiable data they might eventually move in that direction."*

He was very perplexed by what I told him because he came from an environment in which he issued corporate directives and things were done they way he wanted them.

This is common for many people, both new and experienced in franchising. They expect franchised locations to run much like typical corporate locations.

While corporately owned and franchised locations may look very similar on a wall map, that is where the comparison ends.

To be continued...

Welcome to a Very Different Business Called Franchising

Most executives of new franchise systems quickly learn they are in a brand new business - one that doesn't remotely resemble or operate like the successful corporate prototype they started with.

They figure this out in a myriad of ways including:

- Attending franchise events such as the International Franchise Association's annual convention and being overwhelmed with information they don't understand.

- Receiving some expensive legal lumps on the head because of mistakes they've made.

- Pushback from franchisees that don't jump like corporate employees when headquarters bark orders at them.

- By waking up one morning and finding they are totally overwhelmed by the business and wondering *"How on earth did I end up in this?"* and *"What do I do from here?"*

Franchise Mega-Brand's "Best of Class" at Franchise Education - (New Brands)

**FirstLight Home Care®
Jeff Bevis, CFE
President & CEO**

Founded in 2010, FirstLight HomeCare® offers comprehensive, in-home, non-medical and personal-care services to seniors, new mothers, adults with disabilities and others needing assistance. With a presence in over 51 markets across the United States, FirstLight's management team brings more than 175 years of collaborative experience in health care, franchising and senior services, creating the core of FirstLight's foundation.

Franchise Education
Currently over 80% of the FirstLight headquarters' staff are Certified Franchise Executives or enrolled in the program. The deep franchising and operational expertise of the FirstLight Team is in place as a constant resource for franchisee success!

Unfortunately, some never learn until it is too late, and others never learn at all.

Coaching the Team Rather Than Being a Player

Here are two scenarios that compare how franchising vs. corporate-owned locations work:

1. *Corporate Owned Location,*

   I run a test at all the stores I own and it determines that painting the roof fluorescent pink increases sales by 25%. I then order all the roofs be painted fluorescent pink and we see a systemwide sales increase of 25%.

2. *Franchised Locations -*

   As a franchisor, I run the same test on our corporate-owned locations and see the 25% increase. I then share those results with the franchisees at our annual convention. 20% of the early adopters immediately paint their roofs fluorescent pink. A year later at the annual convention, 80% of the franchisees will ask the early adopters if their sales increased. When they hear "yes" from the first 20% then another 60% or so will paint their roofs fluorescent pink. The remaining 20% will wait until they are forced to do so by the Franchise Agreement provisions/renewal or their competitor across the street paints its roof.

Does this mean franchising is bad for new initiatives? Not at all. But, in this example, it does mean that you need a strong periodic remodel clause in your Franchise Agreement and you should start the initiative by engaging the Franchise Advisory Council in the early stages and include a fair number of franchised locations in the test. If you had done that, it would have made a larger impact at the convention and encouraged more people to convert to the new model.

In an earlier chapter I discussed the difference between the macro view of a franchisor and the micro view of a franchisee, which is clearly illustrated in this example. In a non-franchised, corporate environment there is only a macro view - paint the roofs fluorescent pink or else.

As a franchisor you have built and designed a business system (see chapter 10 for more on this) that you have *licensed* to *independently owned and operated franchised locations* (franchisee). As the example proves, this doesn't mean that they will listen or heed everything that you tell or show them.

In order to become an effective franchisor, *or even an effective franchise-headquarters staff member*, you must learn and understand the franchisees' perspective and how it fits into building a brand. I like to use the analogy of a baseball team.

Imagine that as a business owner, prior to franchising, you were a pitcher for a baseball team. As a pitcher, you focused on becoming the best pitcher possible. Because of your narrow focus on pitching, you were not directly involved and did not hone skills for other aspects of the game.

Now as a franchisor, you have become the baseball team coach, which means you must focus on all aspects of the entire team and game. This allows you to do something really cool – watch the plays, coach the players, observe and study the inner workings of the game, and manage game tactics and strategy from the outside in.

As a franchisor (team coach), this "outside the game" perspective allows you to develop the vision, operational systems, technology improvements, training programs, etc. You can then provide leadership to the players/franchisees to *help them execute* the playbook.

If you can **coach** a franchisee to flawlessly execute your playbook, you should have a successful franchisee. Repeat this coaching process with each franchisee and this consistent repetition leads to the by-product of the arrangement - a successful franchisor and system.

The franchisees want to be *trained and coached* on successful methods to build a local business. They expect **the franchisor** to *improve the operational methods and build* the national brand *systematically.*

A Core Ingredient of System Failures

The two top reasons franchise systems fail are undercapitalization and management's lack of franchising experience and knowledge.

While preparing to write *Five Pennies* I had a long discussion with a good friend of mine, Ron Berger, the current Chairman and CEO of Figaro's Pizza®, Nick'N'Willy's®, Sargo's Subs®, and Pizza Schmizza®.

Ron asked me to share a specific story about the first franchise chain he started, called Photo Factory, because it illustrates the devastating effect a lack of franchising experience and knowledge can have on a new system.

Ron started and launched Photo Factory in 1974 and less than five years later he filed both personal and business bankruptcy and closed the doors on the entire company and system.

As Ron puts it, he felt that he knew what needed to be done and did it his way. Unfortunately Ron's way didn't include any franchise knowledge or experience, to which he attributes the failure of the system and the subsequent bankruptcies too.

After that humbling experience he spent the better part of the following year figuring out what to do next and then started National Video, the first national chain of video rental stores. Ron said that the first check written was to join the International Franchise Association (IFA) and learn about the business of franchising.

Months before the annual IFA convention, he would start assembling the issues of his system that he needed to address and when there he would find the people he knew to be knowledgeable on the subjects or attend sessions that addressed them.

Due to this commitment to education and improvement, Ron and his staff grew National Video to be a hugely successful predecessor to the Blockbuster® video era.

Ron, me and countless other seasoned franchise executives sincerely hope that by sharing this story we create urgency, or renew your commitment to continuing franchise education, which is a requirement to becoming a franchise Mega-Brand.

Understanding the Business you're in.

Franchising is a relationship business operating in a regulated environment.

Sounds complicated doesn't it?

Think of it this way — try governing your marriage through a contract. You wouldn't get far, would you? And even if you did, the marriage probably wouldn't last.

Can you imagine $30 penalties for leaving the toilet seat up? Or a $50 game/TV interruption fee? How about a mandatory house-remodel clause every five years? Certainly would make for a tense marriage and interesting reality show, wouldn't it?

While not nearly this extreme, franchise systems are very much like a marriage that is managed through contract and so it is a very delicate balancing act.

> - If you are too easy on governing, the system can get out of control quickly and the problems can be difficult to recover from.

> - If you govern too harshly, the relationship with franchisees suffers and you may be considered a tyrant. The problem can be difficult to recover from.

Seasoned franchise folks understand and know how to recruit, train, coach and grow individual franchisees by molding them into a unified, operating, national brand without getting into legal hot water.

Because of the unique requirements of franchising and growing a national brand, franchise education must become a core element of the company culture.

Franchise Mega-Brand's "Best of Quotes" on Franchise Education

""I see the CFE experience, continual education and expertise gained through the process as a core requirement for leading franchisors."

— Jeff Bevis, President & CEO FirstLight Home Care®

Certified Franchise Executive Program

Officially started in 1991, the Certified Franchise Executive (CFE) program is the unequivocal standard of a robust franchise business education.

The highly recognized designation and program is administered by the Institute of Certified Franchise Executives Board of Governors, a component of the IFA.

To become a CFE you must enroll in the program through the IFA and then earn the required number of credits by attending various franchise education courses and events. It typically takes two to three years to complete and earn the CFE designation.

The Franchise Mini MBA®

Developed primarily for senior management and C-level franchise executives, the Franchise Mini MBA® program is administered and produced by the International Institute for Franchise Education (IIFE) at the H. Wayne Huizenga School of Business and Entrepreneurship at Nova Southeastern University. It provides you the opportunity to delve into franchising at a high level and at the same time earn a large percentage of the credits required for the CFE designation.

The Franchise Mini MBA® program consists of three learning phases that can be taken individually or in combination.

Author's Note: *While the CFE program and Franchise Mini MBA® are the staples of a comprehensive franchise education, there are many more available. For a comprehensive list of franchise education programs and conferences, visit www.FranchiseMegaBrand.com*

Rule Summary

The title of this rule is "Do not have an accountant remove your brain tumor!" While I like my accountant, for obvious reasons, I certainly would not allow him to perform a medical procedure of any kind. While franchise education may not be an obvious component to growing a franchise Mega-Brand, not having it is as serious as the title indicates.

Take the time; get the education; grow your franchise brand the right way.

Key Points

- *Understand you're in a completely different type of business.*
- *Remember to coach not dictate to franchisees.*
- *Not having or acquiring franchise experience can lead to bankruptcy.*
- *Get educated on franchising through the Certified Franchise Executive, Mini MBA and other programs.*

Continued from the beginning of the chapter:

In the beginning of this chapter I told you about a guy who had acquired my competitor and was struggling to understand franchising. He worked hard to learn the franchise business, but after a few years decided that franchising wasn't his "cup of tea" and sold the company to another competitor.

During the time that he owned the system, the number of franchise units in the system fell from around 100 locations to fewer than 30. To his credit, not all of the attrition was attributed to his lack of franchise knowledge. During that same period of time, external market factors contributed to the challenges of the brand. However, solid franchise knowledge would have had a significant and positive effect and lessened many of the external challenges. - *A franchising Mega-Wreck!*

Rule No. 5 – Plant, cultivate, and harvest system best practices.

I was contacted by a prominent franchise attorney who was representing a group of franchisees suing their franchisor because of complacency. The franchisees were trying to create their own national accounts program to effectively manage large customer accounts that they serviced and it was apparent that their franchisor had no interest in helping them with it. The only way to get their franchisor's attention was to initiate a lawsuit.

Their attorney knew that I had extensive experience in establishing and managing national accounts programs and was looking for my perspective as a franchisor.

As a franchisor it seemed very odd and even incomprehensible to me that this franchisor did not want to get directly involved and centralize the national accounts program. After all, it would increase the franchisees' sales revenues and the franchisor's royalty income.

As I soon found out, the lack of interest from the franchisor went much deeper than national accounts...

To be continued...

Franchise Mega-Brand's "Best of Quotes" on Best Practices

"Taking care of the people who take care of the customer is the most important thing you must do."

– Jo DePinto, President & CEO, 7-Eleven®

The Aha Moment of Best Practices

To frame exactly what a business best practice is we will use the example of standard business hours.

Generally most businesses post their hours of operation on the front door of their store, website, and other places to inform customers when they are open. It may seem like common sense to do so, but think of what would happen if they didn't do it.

Imagine how upset customers would be if they weren't able to find the hours of operation on the store's website, and then drove some distance only to find that the store was closed. For this reason it becomes a good (best) practice to post business hours.

At some point in business history this best practice came from a merchant (probably at the urging of his customers) posting his business hours on the front door or window of his shop to inform everyone when he was open for business.

No doubt another business owner saw that sign and, thinking what a clever idea it was, took it one step further by putting up a sign that said "open" in addition to his business hours. Before they knew it, every business had an "open" sign and posted its business hours.

Today we take this best practice for granted, but at one time in business history it was an "aha" moment.

The same goes for making a motel reservation, point of sale systems, the Big Mac®, and, more recently, fast food, dollar-value menus. All of these examples, at one time, were just ideas and are now required business practices in franchise systems.

Creating a Best Practices Clock

One of the reasons business-format franchising has catapulted to today's success levels is the capturing, systemizing, and sharing of best practices throughout the entire franchise system.

Franchise Mega-Brand leaders and staff members instill a culture of continuous improvement in their franchisees and manage it by creating best-practices programs and the communication channels for sharing them.

In short – *"they process the creation of process"*.

To put this into perspective, the Founder of U.S. Lawns® was so committed to developing processes for the company that he even created a special system for sorting staff mail. The team at U.S. Lawns® has never forgotten those days and continues that culture of process today. For that reason, they are named as a Best of Class franchise Mega-Brand.

In the book *Built to Last*, Jim Collins discusses the concept of clock building, which is about building a company than can tick along on its own momentum. Having formalized programs that plant, grow and cultivate best practices within a franchise system produces a clock of continuous brand improvement and prevents stagnation from setting in.

A "Best Practices" Culture Begins at Franchisee Recruiting

As previously discussed in Rule No. 2, franchise Mega-Brands leaders and staff create a culture of codependency with their franchisees.

Developing and sharing best practices is a major ingredient for creating and maintaining strong franchisee relations and it should start before a franchisee even joins the system.

The author Verne Harnish, in his book *Mastering the Rockefeller Habits,* discusses the importance of hiring employees who are aligned with your company's core values. The same principle should be applied to recruiting new franchisees. An emphasis on your system's core values and principles during the recruiting process will attract new franchisees who share the same beliefs.

Developing a list of candidate questions that focus specifically on best practices will help determine how receptive the candidate is to sharing ideas or implementing new processes. You could ask them how they improved efficiencies, or how they have dealt with process change in their previous work experiences. A committee to review franchise prospects can then see how a candidate aligns and may fit in with the system's culture of best practices.

More information on franchisee selection will be covered in Rule No. 6.

Putting Your "Best Practices House" in Order

New-franchisee initial-training should be the aggregate of all your system's best practices, yet I am always amazed how some franchisors allow their training material to become dated.

Ponder these three questions for a moment:

1. *When was the last time you revised your training curriculum?*
2. *Do you know if your training staff is teaching the most current operations and practices in the system?*
3. *Is your training the best that it can be?*

For smaller franchisors that do not have a dedicated training staff, reviewing and maintaining training can be difficult to coordinate with different departments that contribute material and time to creating the training program.

While administrative staff members are most often tasked with assembling and modifying the curriculum and materials, they are not the subject-matter experts.

Therefore, it becomes vital that someone in a management position, with solid franchise operations expertise be responsible for ensuring the training is current, taught effectively, and uses the latest training tools and methods.

If a photo in your training materials shows a guy sporting a 1980's mullet, chances are pretty good that a serious review of them is in order.

Training Huddles

Once someone is made responsible for all training activities regularly-scheduled, "before and after" training huddles should be implemented.

Before every training session, all trainers should meet to review and discuss the current training curriculum and make adjustments to it or the agenda if necessary. At the conclusion

---

Franchise Mega-Brand's "Best of Class" at Best Practices

McDonald's®

**Don Thompson
CEO**

Founded in 2010, McDonald's® is the leading global foodservice retailer with more than 32,000 local restaurants serving more than 64 million people in 117 countries each day. More than 80% of McDonald's® restaurants worldwide are owned and operated by independent local men and women.

Their rich history began with their founder, Ray Kroc. The strong foundation that he built continues today with McDonald's vision and the commitment to keep the shine on McDonald's® Arches for years to come.

of each training session, all trainers meet again to discuss the session and review trainee evaluation surveys (you do have new trainee evaluation surveys don't you?) to determine if any changes or additions should be made.

Regularly scheduled training huddles will provide the rhythm and alignment necessary to ensure that both the trainers and the training are up to date and using the most current teaching tools and methods.

Author's Note: *To download a customizable training evaluation survey, visit my website www.FranchiseMegaBrand.com*

The Importance of "Live" Operations Manuals

If you're an existing franchisor and still utilizing hard copy operations manuals, here's another question for you.

How many of your franchisees can tell you exactly where their manuals are physically located or when they last referenced them?

I'm betting not many of them and it is not because they don't find value in them. Generally it is because the manuals are:

1. *Out of date*
2. *Organized in a manner that makes it difficult to find the required information quickly*
3. *Not readily accessible when needed*
4. *Written like a legal contract - devoid of color, graphics and user-friendly artwork.*

No franchisee wants, or will use, manuals with the flaws I described above. In reality, these four reasons may cause franchisees to stray and create their own version of the franchisor's process. And can you possibly blame them if you were in their shoes?

To have great franchise manuals they need to be an integral part of your initial and on-going training and reflect the franchisees' current, daily operations. In addition, they must be developed and maintained in concert with your Franchise Disclosure Document (FDD). Reviewing your operations manuals in conjunction with your FDD ensures continuity between the documents, and decreases the possibility of conflicting viewpoints between the franchisor and franchisee.

Great manuals should also be fun and easy to use with colors, photos, flow charts, and other graphically-appealing items.

Today's technology allows you to host your new user-friendly manuals online with tab-driven menus which eliminate antiquated PDF's and hard copy binders.

This may create security and proprietary concerns about your intellectual property, but don't be alarmed. There are many security measures which can implemented to prevent sensitive information from falling into the wrong hands. You can tighten security further by dividing the information into general and confidential areas and assigning or restricting access accordingly.

Franchisors are now creating apps that give franchisees direct access to information from tablets and smartphones such as the Apple iPad® and iPhone®. Again, these apps can be very tightly controlled for security.

Not only do apps provide information at the touch of a finger, they can also be customized for individual job functions at the franchisee level. A few staff app examples are: the procedure to create a specific salad, an identification chart for noxious lawn weeds, or the steps taken to ring up a sale.

As more and more Millennials/Generation Y-age people enter the franchising space and mobile computing continues to grow, electronic manuals will not be optional, they will be required.

Because of the importance of operations manuals and their prominent use in a franchise system, I recommend having a reputable consultant that specializes in manual development, design, and creation review them periodically to make improvements and updates.

Franchisee Performance Groups

A Franchisee Performance Group is a group of six to eight franchisees who meet on a regular basis and deep-dive into financial, operational, planning, and marketing best practices. The peer group members also act as an advisory board for their fellow members, holding them accountable for their goals, keeping them committed to the program, and staying focused on improvement.

Benefits to the participating franchisees include:

1. Goal setting
2. Establishing benchmarks
3. Comparing metrics with peers
4. Direct feedback and accountability from peers
5. Peer relationships and support

Rotate the Franchisee Performance Group meetings to each of the member's locations so other members will be able to view the operations and compare them to their own.

Meetings typically last one to two days and each franchisee is given a specific timeframe (usually 30 minutes) to present their business' financial metrics and goals and receive direct feedback from their peers.

Franchisee Performance Groups require a serious commitment from the franchisees and the franchisor as scheduling, time and travel is required.

Because of the depth and analysis of the franchise unit economics that this type of program provides, it is important that participating franchisees be matched with others of similar size and structure. In addition, the chart of accounts for each franchise must be standardized for accurate comparisons between locations.

No franchisee-facilitated program that I am aware of can dive into financial best practices as seriously as Franchisee Performance Groups can; and not all franchisees can, or will participate. However, established Key Performance Indicators (KPI's) from these groups can be published for the entire system to benchmark and learn from.

Franchisee Performance Groups fully embrace and leverage the very reason franchise systems exist – to provide direct networking and sharing of best practices for franchisees to grow their businesses.

For that reason, it is important for the franchisor to establish and help initially guide a group, then step back and let the members direct and manage the group on their own without "big brother" watching.

The results these groups achieve can be astonishing; not only for the members, but for the impact they have on the entire franchise system.

Best Practices Focus Groups Does this requirement go in their contract?

Best Practices Focus Groups are a great system-building tool. They are less intense than a Franchisee Performance Group, but still add tremendous value to the system.

Sometimes structured as a sub-committee within a Franchisee Advisory Council, focus groups can provide direct testing and feedback on specific initiatives such as technology. They can also act as a general group to assemble and disseminate systemwide best practices within a system.

Depending on the size, complexity, and needs of your franchise system, you may have one or many best-practices focus groups including:

- Unit Economics

- Technology
- Products
- Services
- Store Operations
- Area Development/Regional Management
- Marketing and Advertising
- Supply Chain Management
- Green Initiatives

The list can go on and on, but it is completely dependent upon your system's needs.

The frequency with which these groups meet will also depend upon need. Some groups may need to meet once a quarter and others might need to meet weekly, depending upon the requirements.

Franchisees are most often asked to serve or they may have expressed interest in these groups, but they should also be expected to participate for a minimum number of meetings or completion of a term. In my experience, rotating the members of the group every three years helps prevent franchisee "death by committee" and brings in a fresh set of eyes and ideas.

Finally, be sure to thank and celebrate those franchisees that have made the time commitments to serve by formally recognizing them at the annual convention.

Franchisee Interviews

Another excellent tactic for promoting best practices is using the franchisees themselves. Franchisees that serve on Best Practices Focus Groups or are members of a Franchisee Performance Group are always great resources to tap into and usually love sharing their story. Once a month or quarter, host a system-wide recorded webinar/conference call that highlights a franchisee and the implementation of a best practice. Recording and publishing the webinars/calls on your brand's intranet makes these available to those franchisees that were not able to make the call.

Conducting the call or webinar in an interview fashion provides the franchisee the ability to describe the program or process they follow in their own words. Nothing speaks stronger, or is a better testament to implementing best practices than a franchisee telling everyone his story and the results he achieved.

Best Practices Communication and Education Channels

Method	What it Does
Best Practices Showcase Papers	A paper (sometimes referred to as a whitepaper) that highlights a best practice, how it was implemented, and the results that were achieved by it.
Field Representatives & Franchisee Support Coaches	The franchisor's frontline representative who provides support and communication directly to franchises.
Regional Meetings	Smaller, regional meetings between franchisor and franchisee to solicit communications and feedback involving best practices.
Initial & On-Going Training	The on-going training of best practices for existing owners using distance learning, on-site training, and other means. See section below.
Franchisee Performance Groups	See section above.
Best Practices Newsletter	A monthly or quarterly publication that highlights best practices, their results, and how to implement them.
Operations Manuals	See section above.
Franchisee Intranet	The sharing and warehousing of best practices via intranet. See Chapter 9 for more information on intranets and technology.
Annual Convention	The sharing of best practices at the annual brand convention through breakout sessions, round tables, and franchisee showcase.

Franchisee Interview Webinars/Calls	See above section.
Best Practices Focus Groups	See above section.
Franchisee Mentoring Program	A program that provides for successful franchisees to mentor and coach new and current owners on implementing best practices.

On-Going Training Thoughts

If there is one thing that provides incredible value for the royalties franchisees pay and is fairly inexpensive for a franchisor to implement, it is training. Trust me, you can never train enough. I have never ever heard a franchisee say *"Stop, please! I'm over-trained and cannot take one more ounce of it!"*

As franchisees move forward in the lifecycle of their businesses, they will have different training and educational needs. While a new franchisee is focused on marketing and sales to get the business off the ground, an operator who has been open for three or four years is starting to home in on operational and financial efficiencies. Franchisees that have been operating for a long time may be looking to sell or exit their business.

On-going training needs must be continuously assessed and programs tailored to fit these evolving requirements.

Rule Summary

In Rule No. 3 I wrote that every franchisor wants to be McDonald's®. If that is truly your goal then an excellent place to start is studying McDonald's® on how they plant, cultivate, and harvest best practices in their system. McDonald's® is the undisputed king of best practices because they have built an entire company culture around it and continue to improve upon it over 60 years later. If you have this level of commitment to your franchise brand you might very well be on your way to becoming the next Golden Arches.

Key Points

- *Create a best practices clock of continuous system improvement.*

- *Get your best practices house in order.*

- *Organize training huddles.*

- *Develop "live" operations manuals.*

- *Create Franchisee Performance Groups.*

- *Celebrate success through showcasing successful franchise owners.*

Continued from the beginning of the chapter:

Recall my earlier story about the lawyer who represented a group of franchisees that were suing their franchisor because he wouldn't help them organize a national accounts program?

The complacency from the franchisor shouldn't have been a surprise to them at all. I came to find out the franchisor didn't even have or provide an operations manual for the franchisees to operate from. Again... - *A franchising Mega-Wreck!*

Google McDonald's Best Practices

Rule No. 6 – Stack the "entire" deck with strong franchise owners.

I am somewhat well known in franchising and I get calls every once in awhile from people that have something they want to franchise. Recently, a man called who is creating a commercial restaurant/kitchen exhaust cleaning franchise called me. Apparently he'd seen the success that Hoodz® experienced and wanted to get in on the action.

From the moment I was on the phone with him, he was determined to let me know how smart he is. In between his narcissistic rants I asked him if he had a consultant helping him out, to which he proclaimed, *"I can read, and this franchising stuff isn't that hard."* I won't get into the details, but those of you who know me well know exactly what was going through my mind. Biting my tongue, I maintained my professionalism and kept asking questions whenever I could squeeze them in to his monologue. He was writing his own Franchise Disclosure Document and Operations Manuals (he had downloaded from the Internet) and his brother was developing an operating location that would serve as the franchise model.

While he was carrying on about how wonderful he is, he mentioned that the franchise fee would be only $2,000. I managed to ask him if he thought that level of fee would attract the type of candidate he was seeking, and would it cover his cost of supporting a franchisee to a point where their royalties would cover his support costs (royalty break even). While I had my foot in the proverbial door, I went on to explain the principle of "easy in - easy out." That phrase means that without much monetary "skin" in the game people have a tendency to walk away from things. For that reason I suggested that he consider increasing his initial franchise fee to attract a better, financially qualified candidate and cover his new franchisee ramp-up costs.

Based on how the conversation had been going thus far his response didn't really surprise me. *To be continued...*

The Importance of Recruiting the Right Franchisee Team Members

"Expensive Trouble" is the phrase that best describes what happens when you recruit the wrong franchise owners into your system. Trust me (I speak from experience), you do not want any more trouble in your system than you will have on a normal basis.

What? You thought what? Of course you are going to have franchisee challenges. No matter how selective you are and how well you foster positive relationships you're going to periodically hit a bump in the road. The goal here is to minimize the risk of an incompatible franchisee (the bump) and increase the acceptance of a potential superstar by establishing a desirable profile and *"awarding franchises"* to those that match it.

Franchise Mega-Brand's "Best of Class" at Franchisee Selection

BrightStar Healthcare®

Shelly Sun
Co-Founder & CEO
JD Sun
Co-Founder

Founded in 2002 by Shelly & JD Sun, BrightStar Healthcare® offers homecare, (including adult and elder care) childcare (including newborn care, babysitter and nanny services) in addition to medical staffing services for individuals, families and healthcare facilities through over 250 locations nationwide.

The best description I ever heard on the importance of having the right franchisees in your system was from Joe DePinto, the CEO of 7-Eleven® during his keynote at the International Franchise Association's annual convention in 2011.

"When the relationship is good, franchisees can make a bad system succeed. When the relationship is bad, franchisees can make a great system fail!"

While on-going relationships with franchisees can sour for various reasons, what Joe's statement points out is that if you allow the wrong franchisees to enter your system mayhem can ensue. The operational system isn't followed and that leads to declining system revenues, broken system rules, and loss of franchisee profitability, plus the cost of time and money you spend to clean up the mess both operationally and legally.

Now that you know who trouble is let's switch gears and focus on the positive side of this issue.

Brad Pitt Can Help You

I'll be the first to admit that I have made many mistakes in recruiting franchisees over the years, and have had my share of messes to clean up. There isn't a franchise system on the planet that has a *"perfect franchisee cloning system"* or hasn't made a few blunders along the way by allowing the wrong franchise owner or two into their system. Again, the point of the exercise is to <u>minimize</u> these blunders.

Recently a good friend suggested that I watch the movie *Moneyball* starring Brad Pitt as Billy Beane - the real life controversial team manager for the Oakland Athletics.

His words of wisdom to me were, "If you want to learn how to recruit franchisees, watch *Moneyball.*" I am always a bit skeptical about these types of suggestions, but I highly respect my friend's opinion and figured that since I have tried everything else with franchisee recruitment, why not apply a little Hollywood to it?

I must admit, he was right. My approach to franchisee recruitment is forever changed.

I won't repeat the entire movie, but the premise is based on actual events surrounding an extremely small-budget team trying to compete for players against big teams such as the NY Yankee's. It was almost impossible to do, because as soon as he groomed a decent player the bigger teams would pay more money and the player was gone. Hence the term, *Moneyball*.

Having lost one too many players and games, Billy Beane decided that there has to be a "new" way of recruiting players rather than the "old" way of trusting a talent scout's intuition and throwing money around.

If this is starting to sound familiar, it should because as franchisors we have, for years, relied heavily on the "old" way of recruiting franchisees - trusting a franchise sales person's intuition (talent scout) and throwing money at every advertising portal (player salary).

In the movie, Billy Beane runs into a first-year analyst named Peter Brand who graduated from Yale with an economics degree. Peter realized that team managers think of buying A-list players and that many great players with core talents were being overlooked and undervalued for a variety of reasons.

Peter convinced Billy to focus on buying "wins", which meant he needed to buy "runs" and that meant buying "base hits". Billy and Peter made a monumental change in recruiting players and ended up winning 20 consecutive games that year with a bunch of perceived misfits.

The following year the Boston Red Sox attempted to recruit Billy Beane to implement his game-changing methodology. He turned them down and they used his tactics to win the World Series, breaking an 86-year period of losing the series known as the *Curse of the Big Bambino* (Babe Ruth).

Billy Beane forever changed baseball with his methodology. Will you continue the "old" way of selling franchises or will you adopt the "new" way of recruiting them?

So Who Makes a Good Franchisee?

Much like Billy Beane, you have a goal to recruit the best players that will efficiently execute your brand playbook, do it consistently day in/day out and get on base more often and ultimately score frequent sales, profits and system growth – all within your budget. But before you can attain that goal you need to know which traits are the best fit for your brand and operations and, more importantly, which traits are not.

How to Identify & Establish Your Owner Profile

If you have an existing brand with a handful, a dozen or even hundreds of owners, you already know (or had better know) who is performing well within your system. If you're brand is new, don't worry. We'll cover that in the next section.

The key to being an effective franchisee recruiter is to take a defensive posture towards your recruiting efforts. Much like interviewing employees, the objective is to rule out the candidates that do not meet your criteria.

A quick and fast way to start building your owner profile is using the Gazelle Test. Complete the following statement,

"I would rather have 10 of my guy __[their name]__ (the gazelle) than 50 others that would produce a fraction of what he does."

It shouldn't take you long to write down the few franchisees' names that quickly came to mind. Find your system's gazelles and you will have a list of candidate traits to begin building the profile of your ideal candidate.

Franchise Mega-Brand's "Best of Quotes" on Franchisee Selection

"We're going to be partners for 20 years, so it's important we get it right!"

– McDonald's® Franchise Brochure

Recruit For The Attitude & Aptitude - Train For The Results!

Review your system's Gazelle List and define about 10 qualities that make them winners. From there, formulate interview questions that spotlight the desired traits and use them for interviewing candidates.

For example, if one of the qualities you seek is perseverance, ask your candidate to tell you about the most difficult thing he ever did in business and how he managed to get through it. Perhaps he started a new business at one time that didn't make it. Was it because he quit and gave up or were there other circumstances that caused it? Interviewing in this style will tell you something about the candidates' character and if they have the level of perseverance you are looking for.

Perhaps metrics and KPI's are a huge part of your system (if not, they should be). Ask your candidate how they feel about being measured or compared to their peers. Their answers will tell you how, or if, they will function within your system's culture. If they have difficulty with measurement or peer accountability - they should probably go away and cause havoc in someone else's system.

Again, it is important to remember to maintain a defensive posture during these interviews. Ask yourself *"Why should this person NOT be a franchisee in my system?"* or, *"Is there anything wrong with this scenario?"* Remember, the goal is to weed out the incompatible owner.

Once you have developed your new line of questioning immediately incorporate it into your franchise recruiting process and diligently train your entire staff how to use it.

Back to the movie *Moneyball*. Scott Hatteberg had been a star catcher that hit well, threw well, and got on base very frequently. Billy Beane recruited him for his frequent base hits but placed him as a first baseman even though Scott had never been in front of home plate before with balls being hit directly at him. Scott was terrified of the balls being hit at him, but Billy knew that that he could train him for the results he needed from a first baseman because Scott already possessed the other skill sets needed for success. With *proper training and mentoring by seasoned players* Scott turned out to be the great first baseman Billy needed and predicted.

Everyone involved with recruiting new franchisees has to fully understand, and be able to identify, the traits you are seeking. If the candidates don't possess all of the required skill sets (just like Scott) can they be trained for the results? The right owner with the right attitude has the aptitude to learn, achieve and succeed!

Great Idea Lonnie, But I Don't Have ANY Franchisees Yet?

One thing I can assure you is that the franchisees you recruit into your system during the first couple years after startup WILL NOT be the profile of those you will be seeking as your brand starts to emerge and grow.

The challenge as a startup franchise system is that you have no standard by which to measure candidates and at this stage your fledgling system is very entrepreneurial and changing almost on a daily basis.

My advice to you is to find another one of "you" to be your first few franchisees. Because your system is so new, it will take a candidate that possesses an entrepreneurial spirit like yours to be attracted to it. A key recruiting/value point for recruiting another "you" is that person will provide input on operations, development, process, and growing the system, which most entrepreneurial people enjoy doing.

Another method, and not one that I recommend, is affectionately referred to as the "friends and family" program. To get things off the ground, you may have to recruit the people closest to you to help figure out a few things. The problem with this method is that these homesteaders will find themselves feeling significantly out of place as your system grows, matures, and starts putting rules in place. After a few years they may suddenly want to sell or exit their business. This is a normal growth pattern as the profile of the optimum franchise owner changes and is recruited into the system.

Do you remember Tom Feltenstein's book title from an earlier chapter? *Change is Good... You Go First?* The same mantra applies to franchisees. The profile will continue to change and evolve in relation to the growth and evolution of your brand.

BrightStar Care®, a franchise Mega-Brand realized that their franchisee profile needed to change in order to scale from one to multiple units. In the early days of the brand, franchisee selection was based largely on the owner performing an outside sales function. As the brand and model evolved, BrightStar® realized that to effectively scale to multi-units, the franchisee needed to change and have an operational and leadership focus. Proactive annual monitoring of their top performers (gazelles) profile has allowed BrightStar® to make adjustments to their recruiting efforts in relationship to their brand's evolution.

When you suddenly find your franchisees are having difficulty executing the playbook as they should, it is time to review your candidate profile.

Author's Note: *For an in-depth view on the growth of BrightStar Care® and an excellent "how-to" book on starting and developing a franchise, read* Grow Smart, Risk Less *by Shelly Sun.*

You Can't Sell a Franchise - But You Can Help Them Buy One

Okay, here is some straightforward advice: If you have or use the word "franchise" and "sales" combined in any shape, manner, or form whatsoever in your recruiting process, it is time to change.

The term "franchise sales" is very pre-Internet-sounding, old school and <u>wrong</u>. No one (and you know I am right here) wakes up in the morning and thinks, "Today I'm going to go buy a franchise from that great franchise salesman!"

You don't sell franchises. You help people discover, develop and own them and in return they pay you a licensing fee.

Starting a franchised business is too large of a life-changing event for most people to commit to without doing due diligence and completely understanding their obligation. If they skip this they are moving too fast, are too charged with emotion and might make bad decisions. Moving too quickly through the recruiting process is not in the best interest of the candidate, the system, or you as it increases the likelihood that there will be a mess to clean up at a later date because of it.

Creating or modifying your recruiting process to include defensive interviewing techniques based upon your ideal franchisee profile demonstrates to the candidate that you are more interested in them, their success and their fit into your system and culture than their checkbook.

A great example of this is LearningRX®, a franchise Mega-Brand that provides brain training to children and adults with reading and other learning disabilities. I was referred to them while conducting research for this book and what struck me about their brand was that I had to work hard to find the typical franchise information such as franchise fee, startup costs etc., because their entire web presence is geared towards their culture, passion and the community surrounding their brand. Their sole objective is to ensure the candidate is a fit for their culture and values first - *before* they talk about the franchise offering.

Content is Good... Content is Bad...

Franchisee recruiting was simpler back in the 80's, when I was with Super 8 Motels®. There was no Internet, no blogs, no Facebook. Heck, we were just getting used to faxes at the time! Back then when someone wanted information about our franchise opportunity they had to call us and we provided them the information at the speed we desired. That lack of online information allowed our franchise development staff to control the entire process - from A to Z.

Today, with the amount of online content and information that is available, it is increasingly harder to engage candidates because they can discover information about your brand by themselves. While the candidates have stayed fundamentally the same, their exposure to brand information has changed.

They want to be educated before they talk to you or your franchise representative. It is because they know you want to sell them a franchise and they don't want to deal with the sales pressure when learning about your brand. Hence, my reason for dropping the term "franchise sales" and adopting a recruiting approach.

This is one of the reasons why I believe franchise broker networks have become so prevalent. Think about it for a minute: A broker is *"perceived"* as a neutral third party who is not selling anything. They are filtering and advising the candidate on valued options so no sales pressure or tactics are being used.

If a candidate calls you or your development team he is *expecting* to be sold something. In addition to this, professional brokers will take the time to educate the candidate about franchising which also lowers the perceived sales threat level. It is because of the overwhelming sea of franchise opportunities, the mass of information available, the expectation that a franchisor wants to sell them a franchise, and the candidate's increasing need for education and content, that drives candidates to brokers. This makes complete sense doesn't it?

Many systems grew quickly using brokers, while others have had little to no success with them. It all depends on your type of franchise, your offering, and especially how well you work and communicate with the brokers. I am not trying to promote brokers (although I have had overall success with them), but to illustrate the change in candidate behavior.

In the last ten years there has been a major shift in how candidates seek and discover franchise opportunities. They used to begin with discovery and finish with validation and due diligence. Today the socially engaged candidate begins with online due diligence and ends with discovery. They want to find all of the negative things about your system before they even engage with you or your staff. This is not bad but it does mean that you must change the way you communicate your brand messaging.

Free information without selling is the new marketing tactic (like a franchise broker, right?). The old school would call this relationship selling, but it has taken on a whole new meaning with the availability of content and social media. Today franchise brands must churn out information that is directly relevant to the candidate. If the information stays relevant, the candidate will subscribe or opt in to have the information "pushed" to them via mobile technology, social media, or other apps. Once the relevancy is gone so is the candidate.

If there is a down side to the instant availability of content it is that anyone with a "burr under his saddle" about your brand can post it all over the Internet. If your brand is the target of such propaganda the best way to deal with it is by informing your candidates about it up front. Most people can see right through these types of shallow, self-serving posts. But, if your candidate finds it first, it puts you in a position of defending your brand, so it is best to communicate it with candidates as soon as possible.

Overall, the good news about content is that today's candidates are requesting more information about your company than ever before. The challenge for you will be managing it to ensure it is

> *Franchise Mega-Brand's "Best of Class" at Franchisee Selection*
>
> **LearningRX**
>
> **Dr. Ken Gibson**
> **Founder & CEO**
>
> Founded in 2002, LearningRX brain training specializes in treating the cause – not the symptoms – of learning struggles. The programs' game-like exercises and 1:1 trainer-to-student ratios provide guaranteed dramatic improvement in as little as 12 to 24 weeks. With more than 70 centers across the country, LearningRX brain training can help anyone – from 5 to 85 – increase the speed, power or function of their brain. Graduates across the country now see an average IQ increase of 15 points.

relevant to a wide variety of candidates, provides educational benefits and is NOT sales driven.

Managing the Recruiting Process... Or the Lack Thereof

A topic discussed more frequently these days' concerns the franchise recruiting process and how it has been affected by the availability of content and information on the Internet.

As I stated in the previous section, a fundamental change has taken place with candidates and how they investigate franchise opportunities. No longer do they follow the traditional path of discovery or process. When it comes to process, candidates seem to jump in midstream, then are backed up to step one by the franchisor, then ultimately guided back through the franchisor's brand discovery steps.

I have heard stories recently that candidates will call a brand representative and inform them they are ready to enter into a franchise agreement when in fact the company hasn't even talked to the candidate, let alone received an application or disclosed them properly.

Does this affect the recruiting process and the candidate? Who's controlling the process, the franchisor or the candidate? Should it matter? The answers are yes, yes, yes, and yes.

To effectively recruit today a new approach to candidates will require sorting them into two buckets as soon as they enter your system. The buckets are:

1. Incubating Candidates

   These are candidates who want or request formal information on your brand but do not want to speak to anyone yet. An example of an incubating candidate is someone that checks out your website and then "likes" your Facebook page, or follows your brand on Twitter. They haven't supplied you much more than their email address or maybe their name, which may be fictitious.

2. Engaged Candidates

   A traditional franchise candidate is one who jumps into the complete recruiting process right away and is ready to talk and engage.

Has the incubating candidate actually entered your recruiting process? In my opinion, "Yes!" However, the major difference is the lack of engagement and the messaging that is being delivered to that candidate. Remember what I stated in the previous section, these "new" incubating candidates do not want sales pressure or calls but they do want educational information on your brand, so be very careful about *how* the information is pushed to them.

Historically, most franchisors have been very rigid in their recruiting process so the first reaction to an incubating candidate might be, "Come talk to us when you are ready to do something." If this is your position, I can assure you that you are passing over some highly qualified candidates that are genuinely interested in your system.

You must adopt a two-pronged approach to these two different types of candidates. A great example of how this can be accomplished is Great Clips®.

When a potential candidate is reviewing the Great Clips® franchise portal they have two different options to request information. Engaged candidates can opt to complete an online application that routes them directly to the full recruiting process. The incubating candidate can request information on a simple short form that allows them access to a self-discovery tour for more information about the opportunity. If the incubating candidate wishes to move beyond the basic information, they will need to step up as an engaged candidate and fill out the full application.

Adopting a two-pronged approach such as Great Clips® has allows you and your recruiters to focus on the engaged candidates in the pipeline, while you are building a pool of potential candidates that may enter the pipeline at a later time.

To circle back around to the question, who is controlling the recruiting process, the candidate or the franchisor? Again the answer is, "both." Incubating candidates want to (and do) control the process with self-discovery, self-education, and relevant brand information. However, once they make the decision to become an engaged candidate they are typically much more serious about the opportunity and tend to be a more active participant in the franchisor controlled process than others.

This results in awarding franchises to more highly qualified candidates because they have been exposed to more content about your brand's culture, values and mission which they "opted in" to receiving.

New Owner Recruiting Process and Tools

Okay, by now you should know the candidate you want to recruit into your system and how to communicate with them. So how do you manage and fine-tune all of this?

First and foremost you need a process by which to effectively recruit franchisees. All franchise Mega-Brands have some type of a well-defined discovery process and system to manage their candidates. No two of them are the same, however they all follow the same fundamental steps, but not necessarily in this order:

Other things to include
· financing links
· Case studies
· prelim. budget?

1. Lead Sourcing and Aggregation
2. Lead Qualification and Application
3. Brand Discovery
4. FDD Disclosure
5. System Validation
6. Interviewing (including unit(s) and/or headquarters visit)

7. Acceptance or Denial Into the System

8. System On-Boarding

While these steps are basic, formulating a detailed and blueprinted process around them provides you the ability to manage your candidates with great detail. For example, if you have specialized financing, real estate needs or licensing requirements you should incorporate those elements into your process as well. A step-by-step process (aka pipeline) allows you to track exactly where your candidates are within the pipeline, and what their next steps will be.

Franchise-specific technology platforms have made significant advancements in a franchisor's ability to capture leads and manage them. There are a number of customizable, web-based recruiting platforms available with some being standalone systems and others incorporating larger platforms that offer additional franchise system management tools. Some systems also offer more robust candidate-engagement tools such as virtual brochures, candidate-direct messaging, FDD management, and other features. (More on technology will be covered in Chapter 9.)

Pipeline technology tools also help you track and benchmark key metrics associated with the performance of your process, such as lead sourcing, total number of leads, leads to applications ratios, cost per lead, cost per new franchisee, leads to discovery day attendance ratios, discovery day to franchisee conversion ratios, average conversion days, recruiting staff performance, and a myriad of other items. Strong metrics provide not only the data to manage your pipeline, but also direction to *improve* your efficiencies wherever possible. There is also technology available that helps you run security background checks and candidate personality and behavior profiling. When properly designed and implemented these tools can create a robust platform for you to efficiently recruit your optimum franchisee candidate.

Franchisee Recruiting Tools

Tool	Description
Recruiting Process Management	A contact management system specifically designed to track franchise candidates through discovery, FDD disclosure, validation and on-boarding. Some recruiting-process tools have incorporated virtual brochures to immerse and engage the candidate with the brand.
Candidate Profiling	A system utilized for personality and behavior assessment of potential candidates.
Candidate Background Checks	A system utilized for running security background and credit checks on potential candidates.
Candidate Review Committee	A committee that reviews candidates for acceptance or rejection into a franchise system. Review committees are usually comprised of staff members that have interaction with a candidate. It is not unusual to have a few franchisees participate in the reviewing process.
Google, Facebook, and other Social Media	Social media tools are a quick and easy way to conduct background checks and validation on candidates.

Author's Note: For a free list of companies that specialize in franchisee recruiting tools visit www.FranchiseMegaBrand.com.

Two Great Programs for Recruiting Highly Qualified Candidates

Military Veterans (VetFran) - The late Don Dwyer Sr. founder of The Dwyer Group, founded VetFran as a way to say, "thank you" to our veterans returning from the first Gulf war. His daughter, Dina Dwyer-Owens, the past Chairwoman of the IFA, re-energized the program after the Sept. 11, 2001 terrorist attacks. As a component of the IFA, VetFran's ranks have grown to include hundreds of franchise systems that voluntarily offer financial discounts and incentives to veterans seeking to become franchisees.

Veterans and franchising are great matches for many reasons including:

- Demonstrated leadership qualities
- Knowing how to follow and work within a documented system
- Asking for help when needed
- Persevering
- Knowing how to build and manage teams
- Having a "get it done" attitude
- Dedication to the mission.

All franchise companies that participate in VetFran are required to offer the veterans a special incentive. That incentive must be in the form of discounted franchise fees or other types of special financing. Spurred by the success of VetFran, franchisors that are not IFA members have also started promoting veteran incentive programs.

Professional Athletes (PAFI) - Founded in 2010 by Coliseum Enterprises, the Professional Athletes Franchise Initiative (PAFI), in conjunction with the IFA, is a program designed to introduce franchising to professional athletes. Like veterans, professional athletes make great franchisees for many of the same reasons:

- They are team players
- They know how to follow and work within a documented system
- They are financially secure
- They ask for help when needed
- They know how to build and manage teams
- They possess a winning attitude.

Author's Note: For more information on VetFran and PAFI, visit www.franchise.org or www.thepafi.org

Growing Existing Franchise Owners

Franchisors often ask me for advice on growing their system and my first response is always, *"Do you have any strong franchisees that you can get behind and help grow?"* More often than not, I get the response, *"Hmmm, I hadn't thought of that."*

The reasons to assist those franchisees are straightforward: They are already trained and a part of your system, they already understand the brand's mission and culture, and you know their personality and growth potential. However, not all franchisees want to expand or possess the skillsets to do so.

Much like a new franchisee, current ones that are looking to expand into multiple units need to be evaluated on their strengths and weaknesses. For example, a single unit operator may not have the management skills to grow into more stores. A multi-unit franchisee may not have the infrastructure and personnel to grow into more stores.

Use a multi-unit rating system to evaluate existing franchisees on their ability to grow. A formal rating system creates a level playing field for all franchisees, which helps remove any perceived favoritism or emotional decisions.

Franchisees seeking to expand can be rated or scored on their:

- Current and past performance
- Personality and behavior traits
- Financial capabilities
- Current infrastructure
- Management capabilities
- Current and past unit-economics

- Quality assurance and customer service
- Vision for expanding
- Their business plan
- Contingency planning
- Territory availability

Your system may have more or fewer categories than these. Assign scores to each category to determine weaknesses that need to be shored up before taking any action.

Independent Operator Conversions

Expanding your system by converting independent operators can be tricky. Typically, operators that are seeking to convert from independence into a franchise system fit into one of three categories:

1. Lone Wolf Operator

   They are very small and struggling with their current business and may not be financially positioned to convert.

2. Expanding Business Operation

   They are mid-size businesses that are seeking to expand by picking up operational efficiencies and utilizing a national brand name.

3. Mature Business Operation

   The owner has built a sizable business and is looking for an exit strategy or retirement.

While some categories of franchise systems such as hospitality, real estate, convenience stores and home services have grown almost exclusively through successful conversions, this strategy is not for everyone. Conversion franchisees can bring along bad operational habits that are not easy to break, traits that don't fit your profile and also tend to be more entrepreneurial in their thinking.

The recruiting methods typically used to attract new franchisees do not work well for conversions because they are interested in your brand for very different reasons than is a new franchisee. Your messaging and approach need to be very different also.

A conversion growth strategy can be highly successful when planned properly, but it can be a disaster when done wrong. If you are considering conversions for your brand, I highly recommend employing an experienced consultant in this area that can help you create a solid test program before jumping in completely.

Rule Summary

While it may be hard to turn down a candidate that is eager to write a check for your franchise fee, doing so for the right reasons will save you more in headaches than foregoing the fee will. Franchise Mega-Brands take recruitment very seriously knowing that the reputation of the brand is on the line.

You won't get it right every time you recruit a new franchisee, but the goal is to minimize the chance of an incompatible one. As Billy Beane did, define your "base hits" and seek those that fit your profile as closely as possible.

Key Points

- *The goal is to minimize the risk of an incompatible owner.*
- *Be defensive in your recruiting techniques.*
- *Define the "base hits" for you franchisee profile.*
- *Drop the term "sales" and start using "recruiting" methods.*

- *Develop tactics and messaging for both "incubating" and "engaged" candidates.*

- *Use well-defined processes and tools for recruiting and managing candidates.*

- *Remember that strong metrics not only provides you the data to manage your pipeline, but also improve your efficiencies.*

- *Investigate and develop a comprehensive plan for recruiting military veterans and/or professional athletes.*

- *Create a rating system to help existing franchisees grow into multiple units.*

- *Converting independent owners can be tricky. Be sure to test the waters first.*

Continued from the beginning of the chapter:

For the most part, he told me that all he was looking for were "worker bees" in his system and that it didn't matter what type of candidate a low franchise fee would attract.

I certainly hope it doesn't turn into - *A franchising Mega-Wreck!*

Rule No. 7 – Focus on where "the rubber hits the racetrack."

In the mid 1990's Krispy Kreme®, a very popular doughnut chain founded in 1937 and based in the Southeast United States, embarked on a renewed franchise expansion that would take the country by storm.

Krispy Kreme® is best known for their hot *"melt-in-your-mouth,"* glazed doughnuts that are delivered fresh to your hands directly from having a thick sugary glaze oozed on them at the end of the conveyer belt. The store itself is an experience because the entire process is visible from every angle with conveyers carrying doughnuts everywhere. People would line up for blocks at the doors and drive-through windows of stores when the "Hot Doughnuts" sign was lit up. Everybody raved about the doughnuts and the brand assumed celebrity status in the franchising world with its seemingly over-the-top success. Throughout the late 90's and beyond dozens and dozens (pun intended) of Krispy Kreme® stores continued to open up in major markets across the country.

At the time I was still living in South Dakota, which isn't exactly the first place most franchisors think of when expanding, so to get these doughnuts I had to drive a couple hundred miles, which was not a problem with those hot gooey doughnuts waiting for me!

In 2000 Krispy Kreme® went public and quickly became the darling of Wall Street. At the time it seemed that this company could do no wrong.

One day I stopped at a convenience store on the way to the office and found myself staring at a huge Krispy Kreme® doughnut display. I couldn't believe my eyes! How utterly cool! I could now get a box of these doughnuts everyday! I grabbed a dozen and headed for the door. As I was driving, I kept looking at that box and couldn't wait any longer, so I snatched one up and took a bite. That doughnut was terrible! Obviously something was very wrong and that "something" was much, much bigger than my cruddy doughnut. *To be continued...*

This Is Where The Rubber Hits The Racetrack

I often tell my staff members that as a franchisor, we do not make our money when a royalty deposit is received. We *and* our franchisees earn it when the point of sale system rings up a sale for a customer and our job is to help our franchisees ring up lots and lots of them. Losing sight of this leads to fewer sales, frustrated franchisees, frustrated customers, and over time will become a significant branding problem.

I am a huge fan of the CBS series *Undercover Boss* and never miss an episode that is featuring a franchise company. There have been many brands featured on the show and a common thread is how incredibly important "getting in the trenches"

becomes to the undercover boss at the conclusion of the episode.

In fact some of them, such as John Fuller the CEO of Johnny Rockets® who, on the show, worked in the field as a cook, server, and bartender, were so moved by the experience that they mandated corporate staff members to train by working in the field before they can work at headquarters. I applaud John and the others for making that mandate, but it really begs the question, "Shouldn't we have been doing this all along?"

It's common sense that if you work at the home office supporting the system franchisees in some capacity that you learn first-hand what makes things tick.

Franchise Mega-Brands such as McDonald's® have been doing this since the beginning of time and just look where that has gotten them.

Effective Franchisee Support

So what exactly is effective or adequate support for a franchisee? The stock answer is not easily defined because every system will require different levels of support depending on its business model. But, if I were a franchisee I would want a franchisor that is there each and every time that I need help, is committed to my personal growth, treats me as a respected partner, and has a focus on my business profitability.

In table form the statement above looks like this:

Holistic Franchisee Support Model of Success

Responsiveness	The franchisor provides quick and dependable support when needed.
Growth & Opportunity	The franchisor provides personal growth opportunities within and outside the franchise system.
Relationship	The franchisor fosters a sincere and positive relationship but maintains strict system compliance.
Financial Success	The franchisor is committed to increasing unit profits and overall business success.

Responsiveness

You teach franchisees to be responsive to their customers, right? So it is only fitting that as their franchisor you respond to them quickly and dependably. After all, they are paying you a royalty in return for this service and support.

Create standards and protocols in place for your support staff. Define the time allowed for call backs, emails and replies to franchise owners. These will ensure that responsiveness stays high. Not every email or call warrants an immediate return, but they should be handled within a reasonable amount of time depending upon the need. Even when a staff member doesn't have the immediate answer, they should respond and let the franchisee know they are working on finding an answer for them.

The sophisticated technology tools that monitor KPI's, accounting, and other metrics have enabled headquarters' staff to actively monitor the pulse of a unit in "live time" creating what I call, "Just in Time Support." This style of active support allows you to be there when they need you and leave them alone (for the most part) the rest of the time to run their business.

We will cover more about "Just in Time Support" for the franchisee in Rule No. 9.

Growth & Opportunity

Support of the franchisees' personal growth is a support opportunity that is often overlooked. Growth opportunities should be provided both within the system and outside the system. Examples of internal growth include:

- Advisory or Marketing Councils
- Multi-Unit ownership
- Convention planning, Best Practices and other committees
- Leadership, family-owned businesses, exit strategy, tax planning, and other personal educational opportunities.

Examples of external growth include:

- Government-relations opportunities
- IFA membership
- Advisory Boards and other civic and corporate service
- Social activities such as Habitat for Humanity, etc.
- Personal health and exercise.

Relationship

Enough already said on this subject... Please review Rule No. 2.

Financial Success

In addition to the items covered in Rule No. 1, this chapter contains additional, financial-success tools.

Layered Channels of Franchise Support

Franchise-support channels come in all shapes and sizes depending on the makeup and requirements of the brand. Systems whose units produce low royalties or pay a flat fee per unit may not be able to afford a direct channel of field support, but can provide telephone and automated helpdesk support. Larger concepts, with more financial resources, may have deeper and multiple layers of support available.

Regardless of the size or age of your system, a layered approach to franchise support, both personal and automated, is recommended.

The following table illustrates reactive franchise support by resolutions. The solutions change as the needs escalate. For example, the franchisee has a minor problem with his phone system. He first checks out the self-help, automated tools such as FAQ's, which do not resolve it. So he calls his dedicated Business Coach who decides that a technical Subject Matter Expert (SME) is best suited to handle the situation. The SME resolves the problem temporarily, but needs a Field Representative to give him some on-site eyeballs to further diagnose the issue. During a scheduled visit, the Field Rep assists the SME in permanently resolving the problem.

Although this is a simple example, it does illustrate the strength of layered support and its ability to resolve problems quickly.

Layered Support Model

Layer	Types
1. Self-Help Automation	• Operations Manuals • Help Desk FAQ's • Online Intranet Tools
2. Business Consultant/Coach	• Dedicated "GoTo" Rep • In-House or Field • Other
3. Field Support Staff	• Dedicated Traveling Corp Staff • Dedicated Regional Staff • Area Representative • Area Developer • Other
4. Forensic/Subject Matter Experts (SME's)	• Marketing/Advertising • Finance • Accounting • Operations • Real Estate/Construction • Information Systems • Equipment • Other

Polling for Effective Franchise Support

A poll is a very effective tool to measure how your system is performing in relation to franchisee support.

The poll should be conducted at least once or twice a year. All your franchisees should rate and provide feedback about your systems support including methods, staff, and responsiveness.

As brutal as having your franchisees grade you may sound, this is an excellent way to find the problem areas that need to be fine tuned or overhauled completely. Some franchisors frequently poll their franchisees on specific items using their intranet system. While this gives good incremental, anonymous feedback it will not provide you with the comprehensive data that you need to make overall improvements.

Comprehensive polls can be developed for specific geographic areas that will provide feedback for Area Developers, Area Representatives, corporate field representatives, and so forth.

Polls also contribute to positive relations by engaging franchisees, respecting their input and showing you are serious about their overall success.

Author's Note: *There are a number of professional companies that specialize in polling franchisees. They can help you develop and conduct comprehensive polls for your system. For a complimentary list of these companies, visit www.FranchiseMegaBrand.com.*

The Walmart® Blip!

Let's face it, entire books can and have been written about marketing and sales so we will not go into much detail here. If you haven't noticed by now, everyone (and I do mean everyone) has an opinion on marketing, including me.

Putting all of the theories, fluff, opinions, and BS aside, successful franchise marketing is measured by customers spending their money in your franchisees' stores. *No sales = no profits = no royalties = no franchise system. Period!*

The next time you visit Walmart® stop and listen for a minute. The first thing you will notice is the volume of the Point of Sale (POS) systems going "blip" every time a scan is made. It's done for a reason - it is the sound of money and that is where the rubber hits the racetrack for any business. At Walmart® every employee is culturally focused on it.

Compared to non-franchised businesses, franchise companies have multiple channels of marketing to manage, each requiring different messaging and branding, making them a bit more complex to manage. The chart below illustrates these channels using the Walmart® **BLIP!,** which denotes direct customer sales.

Franchisor Marketing Channels

Channel	Description
BLIP! Franchisee Local Marketing	Marketing plans and collateral directly target customers within a franchisee's territory.
BLIP! Franchise System Marketing	Systemwide marketing plans and collateral typically managed in cooperation with National Marketing/Advertising Fund council.
Franchise System Branding	Cause marketing and social volunteer programs.
New Franchisee Recruitment	Marketing plans and collateral targeting new franchise investment partners.

If yours is not a mature franchise brand with dedicated marketing staff, balancing these channels can be difficult. So let me help you focus a little. Use the chart above and my previous statement "no sales = no profits = no royalties = no franchise system" and determine where should you be focusing most of your efforts.

This doesn't mean that you shouldn't put some focus on system branding or franchise recruitment. I am not suggesting that **at all**. But without generating the unit-level profits there will be no capital to fund the other initiatives.

Remember the Walmart® blip and continuously ask yourself and your staff, *"In addition to our franchisees marketing locally for customers, what are we doing as a franchisor to help sound the POS blip at the local level?"*

I can guarantee you that every time you visit a Walmart and hear that sound, you will remember my point.

Reducing Franchisee Expenses

The recent economic downturn put expense reduction front and center for many franchise brands, particularly franchise Mega-Brands. Never before, at least as long as I have been in franchising, has there been such a concentrated effort to improve unit economics.

When prosperous times return many, including franchisees, will again become complacent about controlling and monitoring unit economics. It is a natural tendency – when money flows so does the spending and lack of focus on the detail.

For this reason, it is important that formalized controls are implemented to actively manage franchisees' costs for on-going purchases, real estate and operational expenses. A good, online system with KPIs and metrics will notify you of variances *during* operations, but management of expenses must also be done *before* it impacts the unit level operations

Unit economics should be analyzed on every accounting line-item with the objective of increasing productivity and reducing or totally eliminating costs. Areas of review should include cost of goods sold (COGS), increasing staff productivity, increasing non-staff operational efficiencies, all variable and fixed costs and a comparison of outsourced and in-house costs. On-going, thorough reviews will ensure that franchised units are operating at peak performance with maximum efficiencies.

Underperforming Unit Response Team

If you have a franchisee that is struggling to the point that losing the store is imminent, what would you do?

Depending on the circumstances, a franchisor may deploy a unit response team to assist. Much like a military team, the unit response team is specialized at assessing, correcting, operating and in some cases completely remodeling a franchised location to bring it back to life. The store is saved, the franchisee's morale is restored and their validation of the system is strengthened.

Today, these specialized teams are becoming more important as lenders dig deeper for answers from franchisors about their support structures and how they handle distressed operators.

While you may not have the resources to have a dedicated unit response team standing by, you should have a comprehensive response plan and the necessary resources available to respond to a distressed operator.

Rule Summary

As you can see, I am a firm believer of spending time in the field with customers and franchisees. It's "real" business - a commerce thing. I can't quite get that excitement by being in the corporate office all the time and I hope that you share that feeling.

Never lose sight of the importance of customer sales and your franchisee's cash register. Franchise Mega-Brands have a relentless focus on store operations and driving sales.

Key Points

- *Spend time in the field – it pays huge dividends.*
- *Provide holistic support opportunities to your franchisees.*
- *Provide layered support to your franchisees.*

- *Use polls to measure your support performance.*
- *Remember the Walmart® blip!*
- *Assist franchisee profitability* by reducing expenses and increasing efficiencies.
- *Create an underperforming-unit response team.*

Continued from the beginning of the chapter:

My cruddy doughnut experience was the beginning of a huge downturn for Krispy Kreme®. They had become a victim of their own success and lost focus on what had gotten them to where they were.

They had embarked on a massive expansion of delivered packaged doughnuts to convenience stores, grocery stores and many other channels as a growth tool. This distribution tactic resulted in a significantly diminished quality of the product because the doughnuts were simply not the same as the ones that came off the conveyor belt. The packaged doughnuts were, for the most part, day-old and had lost the hot, gooey appeal and mystique that customers came to expect.

This over-extension of the franchise brand and loss of product quality led to diminished sales, store closures and a hard beating on their stock price. It still haunts the company today.

Will Krispy Kreme® make a comeback? It is hard to tell, but remember the lesson: Never, EVER lose sight of what makes a franchisee's cash register sing. *- A franchising Mega-Wreck!*

Rule No. 8 - Create partners in growth.

Last year a close friend who has been in franchising for many years sent me an invitation for an event geared toward independent, home-services contractors. He had been consulting with the host company and wanted me to attend to see what he had discovered while working with them. I went because a private equity firm that I work with from time-to-time had an interest in acquiring them and this event allowed me to do some due diligence.

This company was very successful and I was excited to attend the event and learn how they were soliciting conversions of existing contractors into their franchise system. So off to the event I went.

I was very impressed with how the presenters painted a picture of their industry, their company's relative size and scope within that market and their vision for the future. They provided excellent, professionally-developed learning materials from which they taught the approximately 30 attendees how their independent businesses could be improved and revenues grown significantly by using tools that were available only to the big brands. They provided details on all of the programs in their system such as call accounting and scheduling software, financial metrics tools, purchasing power, operational methods, marketing and advertising, and more. The entire program was exceptionally well scripted and well presented. Yes, this company definitely had its act together! During the breaks, I networked with many of the contractors and felt that many arrived as independents, but would be soon become franchisees of the company.

As we reconvened in the meeting room, I was expecting everyone to be disclosed with the company's FDD, but something totally unexpected blew me right off of my chair!

To be continued...

The Importance of Creating Partners in Growth

If you think about it for a minute, any major franchise such as SUBWAY® Restaurants, Super 8 Motels®, 7-Eleven® or other well-known brands, carry some history and have evolved to represent something much more than an ordinary franchise system.

That "something more" is going well beyond the standard business of licensing locations by developing growth programs and/or tools that positively impact the entire system (such as national partnerships, accounts, or other macro-level programs). While it may seem that the scale of the franchise would naturally drive these types of programs, they are often under-developed elements.

When properly designed and executed, these programs can be powerful catalysts that turn a run-of-the-mill franchise into a franchise Mega-Brand.

Franchise Mega-Brand's "Best of Class" at Creating Partners in Growth

Super 8 Motels®

John Valletta, CEO

Dennis Brown
Ron Rivett
Co-Founders

The name is synonymous with interstate travel. Everywhere you go - you will see Super 8 Motel's® logo on interstate exit signs.

Founded in 1972, Super 8 is the world's largest economy lodging chain with over 2,100 properties in the U.S., Canada and China. Super 8 has recently launched a brand refresh with a new logo and a fresh, new interior and exterior design program.

Guests can depend on every Super 8 to deliver on the brand's "8 point promise," which includes complimentary SuperStart® breakfast, free high-speed internet access, upgraded bath amenities, free in-room coffee, kids under 17 stay free, and free premium cable or satellite TV.

A Story of "Something More"

I, quite literally, grew up with Super 8 Motels®. As a youngster in my early twenties, I joined the company in franchise operations and spent eight years helping grow one of the largest and most iconic brands in the United States today. I am very proud to have been a part of it.

While we may not have realized it at the time, Super 8 Motels® implemented two distinct initiatives that set us considerably far apart from the competition, generated tremendous revenues for our franchisees, and were quite visionary.

Those initiatives are the national reservation system and the V.I.P. customer program. During the 1970-80's it was unheard of to have an in-house reservation system as most lodging chains outsourced their reservations to companies that specialized in that process. The V.I.P. Club, better known today as a "loyalty program" was even more advanced and visionary for its time. Today, programs such as these are taken for granted and used by countless numbers of businesses in varying sectors. As you might expect, both of these programs were more happenstance than strategically planned initiatives, but smashing successes none-the-less and still thrive today.

Let's examine them as they are perfect examples of franchisor-sponsored initiatives that benefited all franchisees and created partners in growth.

Superline® - The Super 8 Motels® National Reservation System[1]

In 1974 the very first Super 8 Motel® was built in Aberdeen, SD and in 1975, the toll-free national reservation line was launched and handled by a single operator. She would receive the call from a guest, write the reservation down on a scrap paper, and then call the motel to book the room.

Starting in 1977, the system was named Superline® and was upgraded to a large wheel with hundreds of slots that spun in a circle. Operators on one side would receive the reservation and then stick it in a correlating slot for the motel. Operators on the other side would spin the wheel, pull the form and call the motel to book the room. Believe it or not, this was a highly efficient system.

By the early 80's the daily call volume was exceeding a 1,000 reservations per day and a computerized system was required. By the end of the 80's over 325,000 calls per month were coming through Superline® and being dispatched directly to franchisees properties.

Super 8 Motels® was the first national, economy-lodging chain that offered a centralized toll-free reservation line. Not only did Superline® generate direct revenues to franchisees, it was also a tremendous value proposition for joining the system.

The Super 8 Motels® V.I.P. Club[1]

Another program that benefited franchisees and created partners in growth was the launch of the Super 8 Motels® V.I.P. card in 1977. It was initially conceived by then brand-President Dennis Bale after he noticed another motel that had a frequent customer program. The V.I.P. program was launched with nothing more than applications at the motels. We completed a credit check on the applicant and he received a paper card that was typed out with their name, address, and member number. Yes - this was all done with a typewriter.

V.I.P. members received a 10% discount off rates at participating locations and could cash checks at those properties. The program grew like wildfire, and within a few months the membership count was over 1,000. By 1983 there were over 60,000 members, and in two more short years, the count had grown to over 207,000 members and was gaining speed. Not many years later the count was over 6 million people.

The guests that carried these cards were people who stayed frequently at franchisees' properties and were fiercely loyal. This program, along with Superline®, played a major role in the success of Super 8 Motels® and continues that success today.

Author's Note: *I still have my original V.I.P. card. Back in the day, Super 8 corporate staffers carried special-issue cards that had a denotation of "S8" with a corporate number on them. I always got a chuckle when desk clerks would get extremely nervous after they noticed my number at check-in. On another note, I also know the whereabouts of the wheel that was used in the early reservation center. Wouldn't that make for an interesting conversation piece?*

While not every franchise brand may have opportunity to create industry-changing programs such as the V.I.P. Club or Superline® there is opportunity for every brand to make great innovations. Spending time discussing think-tank level innovation with your franchisees, customers, staff, suppliers, and stakeholders is bound to produce a multitude of ideas that can be implemented into your "Model of Success" strategic plan and developed into fantastic programs for your system.

National Accounts Programs

National Accounts programs are mostly associated with services and products and have been around in some variation nearly as long as franchising has. National Accounts customers are companies that are typically larger than any single franchisee can service, have specific pricing or account management requirements, or are spread out over significant geographic territories.

National Accounts epitomizes the scale that franchising affords and can be a tremendous revenue generator for both franchisees and the franchisor. Many potential franchisee candidates have come to expect these programs from the sophisticated franchise brand they are investing in. Because they bring a sense of validation and prestige to the brand (even though not all franchisees will benefit the same from the program), a National Accounts program can be great sales tool for recruiting new franchisees.

Do not let your franchisees get too dependent upon your National Accounts program and not adequately develop their local markets. It can be a disaster if the National Accounts customer abruptly drops its contract or sales volume, leaving the franchisees to scramble for sales of their own. Franchisees must understand that National Accounts customers can come and go and the revenues they produce should be used to augment their own efforts.

The National Accounts program must be transparent and done in partnership with your franchisees or it will be the proverbial can of worms for you. When franchisees believe their franchisor is driving revenue only for increased royalties or processing fees rather than for their unit profitability, issues such as territorial encroachment, refusing work, payment disputes, sub-contractors issues and others can manifest themselves within the National Accounts program.

It is best to build a National Accounts program into your franchise system from day one and allow it to grow and evolve with the brand. If you want to introduce a new National Accounts program into an existing system, my advice is to engage a

Franchise Mega-Brand's "Best of Class" at System Partnerships

Abrakadoodle®

Mary Rogers
Rosemarie Hartnett
Co-Founders

Founded in 2002 by award-winning educator/franchise developer Mary Rogers, CFE, MA.Ed, and children's services franchising expert Rosemarie Hartnett, CFE, Abrakadoodle® is the most comprehensive creativity and art education company of its kind, offering extensive visual arts classes, camps and parties for children ages 20 months to 12 years old.

Abrakadoodle's® programs inspire children's imaginations by immersing them in such art forms as painting, sculpting, mosaics, collage, digital photography, paper and fabric art, stamping, sketching, anime, studio art, foil embossing, and more. Abrakadoodle® has received seven First Place Awards from Nickelodeon's® Parent Picks Awards for "Best Art Program to inspire your child's inner Picasso." Abrakadoodle® also received two Parents' Picks awards for "Best Kids Party Entertainer" and "Best Kids Party Place."

reputable consultant that has experience in this area. Work with your legal counsel to review and structure the program. No shortcuts can be taken in this area, because an improperly designed National Accounts program can quickly cause sour relationships with your franchisees and prompt legal disputes.

Done properly, a National Accounts program can significantly enhance franchisee relations, unit profitability, and propel a franchise system to national status.

Author's Note: *For a comprehensive legal paper on National Accounts developed by the ABA Forum on Franchising visit www.FranchiseMegaBrand.com.*

Strategic System Partnerships   *local clean ups*

In conducting research for *Five Pennies* I was very surprised that I didn't find much information about strategic partnerships in franchising. After all, partnering is very common in franchising and when done properly can put a brand "on the map".

Brand partnerships come in all shapes, sizes and varieties, but the most important thing about them is that they need to be a good fit that helps both partners grow and succeed.

Some Success Stories

When I was the CEO of Ident-A-Kid®, we formed a partnership with Child Rescue Network, a nonprofit that specializes in providing child safety education, training, and certification. The partnership allowed our Ident-A-Kid® franchisees to provide free, child-safety education and training in their local communities.

For Ident-A-Kid®, this program further promoted our cause and established our franchisees as child-safety experts within their community. It ultimately helped our franchisees sell more Ident-A-Kid® cards, increased their profitability and had strong ROI for the entire system.

It furthered the Child Safety Network cause and promoted their brand at a national level. As a non-profit, they depend on monetary donations to survive, and the Ident-A-Kid® franchisees promoted that as well. The program was widely embraced by Ident-A-Kid® franchisees and continues to grow.

Another partnership success story is Abrakadoodle®. Founded by Mary Rogers and Rosemarie Hartnett, Abrakadoodle® provides art education to children. As a startup in 2002 the brand was very small but they had big dreams and somehow convinced Crayola® to form a national partnership with them. It was remarkable to see a company the size of Crayola® partnering with a much smaller, start-up company with fewer than 10 locations, such as Abrakadoodle®.

The partnership called for Abrakadoodle® franchisees to use Crayola® products exclusively. This was a small price to pay for the national media attention it brought. The validation and association with Crayola® also benefitted their franchise recruiting efforts. Their successful relationship with Crayola® continues today and for that reason they are featured as a "Best of Class" franchise for system partnerships. It just goes to show that no matter what size your company, successful partnerships can be built.

Types of Partnerships

Partnerships can be developed in almost every piece of your franchise business; it just takes a little elbow grease and creativity. Here are some examples to consider:

- Healthcare and medical facilities
- Lead referral sources
- Suppliers, equipment, or product sponsors (e.g. Crayola®)
- Insurance companies
- Associations
- Joint selling opportunities
- Cause marketing (i.e. Child Rescue Network)

- Partnering with non-franchised companies
- Other franchise systems
- Almost anything you can leverage with someone else

7 Elements of a Successful Partnership

Partnerships only work as well as they are developed and managed. To create a strong lasting partnership they must be:

1. Championed

   A senior level executive from both companies must get behind the partnership and promote its success.

2. Documented

   A great program will be spelled out, documented in a manual, and distributed to all franchisees for reference.

3. Trained

   Once documented, all franchisees must be trained on how the program works and how to best use it.

4. Managed

   The program must be managed to ensure that that it is successful and continues to operate as planned. Reviews should be conducted periodically to ensure that goals are being met.

5. Celebrated

   If it works, toot your horn about it! Celebrate franchisees that make a success out of it. This creates press and media opportunities for both companies.

6. Integrated

   Both companies need to embrace the partnership equally or it will not reach its full potential. There must be regularly scheduled communication between the parties.

7. Mutually beneficial

   All parties (the partner entity, franchisor, and most importantly franchisees) should win from the partnership. The goals and benefits should be established for both parties to understand what you want to achieve with the partnership.

A great partnership can be a tipping point for a franchise brand, however it's important to ensure that it's structured properly. A poorly designed partnership will provide just that - poor to no results and will quickly be forgotten about by franchisees, the franchisor and the partner alike.

Franchise Mega-Brand's "Best of Quotes" on Creating Partners in Growth

"You can't have a successful franchisor without successful franchisees and you can't have successful franchisees without a successful franchisor."

– Bill Rosenberg, Founder, Dunkin' Donuts® & International Franchise Association

---

Rule Summary

If you truly want to create a strong national brand it's imperative that you formulate programs that go well beyond issuing franchise agreements. Franchisors that do not create partners-in-growth programs may be more likely to stall and reach a plateau, causing the system's growth to stop.

By talking to your franchisees, stakeholders, suppliers, executive team, advisers, customers and anyone that comes in contact with your brand and using a little creativity, ingenuity, and vision, ideas will develop that help foster strong partnerships and national accounts which will grow.

Key Points

- *Determine and develop programs like Superline® and the V.I.P. club for your brand.*

- *Do you have a national accounts program? Do you need one?*

- *What types of strategic partnerships do you have?*

- *Have you implemented the 7 Elements of a Successful Partnership?*

Continued from the beginning of the chapter:

As all of the attendees filed back into the room and started taking their chairs - the staff members started handing out materials that outlined costs associated with each of the different services or products that they could purchase.

For quite a while I was very confused and wondered what was going on because I was expecting them to be handing out FDDs and other recruiting materials. To my absolute amazement, and what blew me off my chair, was their "a la carte" style. The independent contractors could purchase the exact same services, tools, software, purchasing, marketing, and training that the franchisees got. Everything! Without being a franchisee! In reality, one of the company's existing franchisees could drive by an independent competitor located a block away, and that independent was benefitting from the exact same resources as the franchisee, with the exception of the brand name!

Competing with your own franchisees is certainly not creating partners in growth - and doing so will ultimately land you in hot water with your franchisees. This is... *a franchising Mega-Wreck still waiting to happen!*

Rule No. 9 – Manage your system like NASA would.

I have started every other chapter with a story about a company that became a Franchising Wreck. For this chapter I am going to put a little different spin on it by telling you the story of three spirits, the ghosts of technology past, technology present, and technology future.

We'll begin with the ghost of technology past. In the 1990's I founded and owned a franchise brand named Computer Doctor®. We had retail service centers that provided computer repair and sales, but our core business was technology repair. Computer Doctor® expanded quickly across the country and during that time we rapidly grew our national accounts' division to include large retailers whose point of sale (POS) systems we serviced. For those of you who are not technical, a POS system is an electronic cash register.

One of those accounts was Kmart®, which was doing quite well at the time. We warehoused massive amounts of their IBM® POS equipment. These systems were very heavy, enormous and becoming antiquated, even back then. Whenever a problem popped up at a store we would dispatch our POS engineers to clear it up. Kmart® was an excellent account and paid well, as you might imagine. *To be continued...*

Let's move on to the ghost of technology present. By the early 2000's we had grown beyond Computer Doctor® and launched a major B2B technology-franchise called Expetec®. During that time major shifts in the technology services sector were happening .There were many computer repair competitors in our space, and more seemed to sprout up overnight.

Our company was already moving out of computer repair (aka break/fix) and into a remote-services business model. It was during this time that I called a Board of Directors' meeting to tell them about a company that had developed a disruptive business model that would forever change the computer break/fix world. I had been keeping my eye on this company for some time and felt that we either needed to form a partnership with them or acquire them. Not only would this company be a game changing fit for us, but it would severely impact the viability of other franchised competitors. *To be continued...*

Finally, there's the ghost of technology future.

As fast as the tech-franchise sector grew in the 90's, the healthcare franchise brands are growing now. New brands are popping up on a daily basis and it is getting harder to know which is which because there are so many of them.

Franchise Mega-Brand's "Best of Class" at Technology Implementation

TWO MEN AND A TRUCK®

Brig Sorber
President & CEO
Mary Ellen Sheets
Founder
Melanie Bergeron
Chair

TWO MEN AND A TRUCK® is the largest franchised moving company in North America. It includes more than 220 locations and more than 1,400 trucks on the road. Each location is independently owned and operated, and sells boxes and packing supplies. Locations complete home and business moves, as well as packing and unpacking services.

Technology plays a huge role in the success of these brands because they use software development to assist in the management of scheduling, billing, licensing, medical, non-medical, insurance claims, HIPAA, and a myriad of other moving pieces that must be tracked, analyzed, recorded, and highly secure. In short: these are very sophisticated businesses with very sophisticated technology requirements.

I have a personal interest in this franchising sector and have been studying many of the players in this space. I have determined that, for the most part, there are three camps concerning their technology usage: Franchise brands using off the shelf software applications, Franchise brands using modified off-the-shelf software applications, and Franchise brands building extraordinary software applications from the ground up. The implications of these technology decisions may play a huge part in the long-term success of these brands. *To be continued...*

The Importance of Managing Your System like NASA

A Morgan Stanley Internet Trends Study states that mobile technology is growing faster than any other industrial or technology segment has ever grown in human history. I recently contributed to an article in QSR Magazine® about McDonald's® foray with localized, digital TV in their restaurants and believe my quote sums up the reason why your franchise brand must embrace technology at every level.

"If QSR is to compete, it will need to shift its communications methods to those of its customers. If not, those customers will find alternatives and tweet about it until the cows come home."

Not only should the restaurant sector be concerned about shifting consumer communications, but every franchise sector should be concerned as well. Franchise brands do not have the luxury of determining whether they should be interactive or not, as the customer is truly driving the demand, and that customer list includes your franchisees. If the great recession taught us anything it is that measurement of franchisee metrics in real time is no longer a choice; it is a requirement.

A Changing IT Structure

To remain competitive in your franchise category, you need to be continually investing into new technology. A few years ago noted author and technologist, Scott Klososky, at the IFA's Executive Leadership Conference, spoke of the concept of "geek seeding" departments for social media application. While that is a good step in the right direction, it leaves a top-down hierarchy concerning IT, which hasn't evolved as quickly as the technology that is being managed.

To take Scott's concept further I advocate that old-style, dedicated IT departments should be flattened out through your entire organization by "geek seeding" all departments because old-school, centralized IT departments are built to be *reactive*. A flattened "geek seeding" approach puts the expertise at the front lines, to better see where technology efficiencies can be picked up and seek specific technology engagement in new operations. In addition, response times for any technical problems are much, much quicker. This approach pushes technology needs and issues upstream to management for the appropriate decisions.

Just as technology is changing, so too must your internal IT structure.

Managing Costs

While the hard costs of technology have decreased dramatically in recent years, the increased soft costs of integration and additional investment into new platforms such as social media tools, mobile technology, and others have kept technology investments towards the top of expenditures. If not, they should be if you are to remain competitive in your market space.

Work with your accounting team to determine the proper financial allocations you should be making for annual technology upgrades. If you have a technology fee as part of your Franchise Agreement's fee schedule, review it to ensure it is an adequate amount to finance any annual technology upgrades. If the current amount is not enough, discuss this thoroughly with your legal counsel to understand your Franchise Agreement's contractual limitations before making any decisions or adjustments to this fee. Anytime there are discussions concerning fees or technology changes it is important the Franchisee Advisory Council or technology committee be involved with these decisions. Nothing can lead to system contention faster than forcing additional costs or technology on to franchise owners without their involvement and buy-in.

Proper planning, your franchisees' input, and exercising patience while planning, can make technology changes or upgrades go much smoother.

> **Franchise Mega-Brand's "Best of Quotes" on Franchisee Metrics**
>
> *"The numbers don't lie."*
>
> *– Mary Ellen Sheets, Founder, Two Men and a Truck®*

The Layers of Franchise Technology

There is so much depth and detail concerning technology that it would be impossible to cover in an entire book, let alone this chapter. My focus here is to make you aware of the importance of technology in your brand and mindful of the areas that you must monitor and measure. To make it a little easier to understand and digest I have itemized franchise technology needs and/or requirements in the following table.

Many technology requirements, such as franchise unit-level KPIs, are multi-layered. For example, the franchisees' unit-level KPIs need to be reviewed by the franchisees, rolled up to the franchisor and interpreted by various departments such as marketing, training and field support.

Keep in mind that not all franchise systems have the same technology requirements as listed below, and some may have additional requirements or needs that are not included. Many of these items might run on the same technology platform as your intranet or POS system, but individual modules still need to be customized and developed within these systems.

While this is not an exhaustive list, I have attempted to include as many franchise brand technology items as possible.

Franchisee Unit, Customer, & Franchisor Technology Requirements

Point of Sale (POS) w/Payment Methods	Payroll
Accounting	Inventory Management
Supply Chain Management/Fulfillment	E-Commerce Systems
Sales Benchmarking KPI's	Chart of Accounts KPI's
Labor Efficiency KPI's	Customer Service KPI's
Dispatch & Scheduling	Customer CRM, Net Promoter Systems
Communication Systems (VOIP, Email, Call Accounting)	Integrated KPI Dashboard Including System Rankings, Goals, Balanced Scorecard, Market Share, etc.
Digital Reservation, Menu, & Ordering Systems	Unit Operations/Production Systems
Other Measurements i.e. Conference Attendance, Training & Education, Compliance, Mystery Shop, Government Relations, Cause Marketing, etc.	Quality Assurance, Health/Medical, and/or Licensing Requirements
Brand Intranet (Franchise Relations, Support, Helpdesk, & Electronic Communication)	Staff Communications/Drive Thru Systems
Smartphone Apps	Customer Marketing Systems i.e. Social Media, Email Marketing, Ad Creation, etc.
Internet Hotspots	Search Engine Optimization (SEO)
Product & Franchise Recruiting Websites, Blogs, Landing Pages, Unit Locator, Localized Zee Websites	Pay Per Click Advertising (PPC)

Online Video	Online Advertising
Customer Geo-Mapping/Targeting	Aggregate Systemwide or Geographic Specific Metrics
Franchisor Accounting Systems	Restaurant & Services Listings Software i.e. Angie's List, etc.
Franchise Recruitment/Lead Generation & Management	Training Systems
Real Estate	Legal Compliance
Franchisee On-Boarding	Territory Mapping
Royalty Reporting Systems	Corporate Locations Systems
Franchise Operations Manuals	Internal Operations i.e. Email Systems, Phone, IM, Centralized File Storage
Energy Control & Security Systems	

Put a Technology Policy in Place

I strongly recommend that you include your technology policy in your operations manual. This has been made even more important in light of the rapid growth of social media. That requires franchisors to implement, manage, and monitor technology and the social media messaging. I can't stress enough the importance of monitoring and maintaining your online brand reputation.

Social media platforms such as Facebook, Twitter, Yelp, LinkedIn, YouTube and scores of others have given everyone a public and viral platform from which to broadcast both the good and bad about a brand. So the task of managing brand compliance with franchisees, their public personas, and reaction to negative criticism becomes very important.

If you don't already have a technology policy in place; engage your legal counsel and social media experts right away to develop a comprehensive policy for your brand. It is important that you provide your franchisees with the tools and guidelines concerning social media before they develop their own. The last thing you want going viral on the Internet is a poor brand message, right?

Brand/System Intranet

One of the most affordable franchise management tools is an intranet. Whether you are a new or developing franchise system, Brian Spindel, Co-Founder and President of franchise Mega-Brand PostNet® advises this is where you plant your initial flag with franchise technology.

Brian and his partner and CEO, Steven Greenbaum, co-founded PostNet® in 1993 and made remaining on the forefront of technology a core piece of their growth strategy. They started with a simple intranet and went completely online (paperless) in 1999. Today the entire franchise system uses cloud-computing apps. In keeping pace with technology development, all of PostNet's® online presence is optimized for mobile devices, not only setting the example for other franchise brands to follow - but also for their core customer, which are home-based and small businesses.

There are a number of reputable specialists that provide franchise system management intranets. They are not all equal in the tools and components they offer. While some provide the basics such as system email, franchisee communications, and a document library system, others provide a complete platform for franchisee recruitment, store opening, franchise compliance, royalty reporting, fulfillment, marketing, advertising, and much more. Many of the items listed in the technology chart above are available, or can run on these platforms saving the franchisee and franchisor time, money, and aggravation by providing all system tools centralized with one login for access, ease of training, and reduced administrative costs. These systems run on remote and secure hosted sites, which means you and the franchisee have minimal to no hardware costs at implementation.

But, I have seen companies make the mistake of spending the time and resources needed to implement a robust brand intranet, then promptly ignoring it by not having a dedicated administrator managing it, maintaining postings and content, or training franchisees.

For an intranet to be successful it must become as much a part of the brand culture and requirement as the Point of Sale system. It has to be trained, used, and promoted as a departmentalized franchise system tool. This type of technology implementation can sometimes be a difficult change for franchisees that have been in a system for a long time, but they must understand and adapt to it in order to stay relevant. Like any change, you will find those that will jump in right away, some will wait to see how the early adopters do with it before they jump in, and then others that may have to be forced into adopting it.

As discussed earlier in this chapter, programs can be designed to assist franchisees in embracing and implementing technology on a systemwide basis by working directly with your Franchisee Advisory Council or a dedicated Franchisee Technology Committee,

The larger your franchise system is the longer it will take to implement a system intranet, so make patience and on-going communications with your franchisees your top priorities. It is not uncommon to take two or three years before a new system intranet becomes a normal part of everyday business for everyone.

Author's Note: *For a list of system intranet suppliers, visit www.FranchiseMegaBrand.com*

A Story of Success

Mary Ellen Sheets was not only a computer systems analyst she was the founder of Two Men and a Truck®. Her attention to detail in the area of analysis helped Two Men and a Truck® start as the first and only franchised moving company and grow to be the fifth largest moving company in the nation.

While you might be wondering how much can really be measured in the moving business, let me assure you that measurement with Two Men and a Truck® extends well beyond the business of moving a couch. KPIs have been established for almost every business function and interaction with the franchisor and customer, including conference attendance, training and education, customer satisfaction, and government relations, to name a few. These KPIs are not only measured and included in the franchisees' overall benchmarks of performance. All measures are shared transparently with all other franchisees in the system. This balanced scorecard approach to system management has resulted in impressive growth in their system. Two Men and a Truck® continues to invest heavily in their information systems, transforming a seemly mundane trucking business into an organization that is as highly technology sophisticated as they come. Because of this, I have named them a "Best of Class" franchise Mega-Brand at technology implementation and a model for others to emulate.

Franchise Mega-Brand's "Best of Class" at Technology Implementation

PostNet®

Steve Greenbaum
CEO & Co-Founder
Brian Spindel
President & COO
Co-Founder

Founded in 1993, Denver-based PostNet® has more than 800 locations worldwide, including several hundred in the United States. Each PostNet® Neighborhood Business Center specializes in meeting the graphic design, printing, copying and shipping needs of businesses and busy consumers, with a focus on exceptional, personal customer service. PostNet® centers offer full-service digital printing; full- and self-service copying; document binding and finishing; and services like graphic design, computer rental stations, private mailbox rentals and more.

Just in Time Support

In an earlier chapter I discussed *"Just in Time Support"*. This style of proactive support allows you to be "there" when a franchisee needs you and leave them alone to run their business (for the most part) the rest of the time. However, *Just in Time Support* can only be used when the proper technology systems are in place and a standardized systemwide chart of accounts is adopted. You do have a standardized chart of accounts for your system, right?

To make it work robust KPIs and their percentage margins must be established for all unit-level, operational items. Then you can monitor fluctuations. A good example of this is labor costs. By using a basic color-coding system (green for good and red for bad) when labor costs hit the red zone, franchise support personnel will be alerted to contact the franchisee to discuss the issue and help them make changes to correct it.

Think of it as the title of this chapter states, while the astronaut is busy managing their operation, Houston is monitoring the systems and helping make corrections.

To become a franchise Mega-Brand, you will need to establish and provide *"Just in Time Support"* by managing your system like NASA would.

How Far Should You go with Technology

Do you want to be a technology company? My technology background makes this a fair question to ask. The reason is simple: If you develop technology systems in-house or have proprietary systems that are co-created with in-house technologists, you reach a point where you have essentially grown a technology company within your franchise organization.

A word to the wise: Just as you needed to get franchise education to be in the franchising business, you must also hire people who understand this piece of your business. Everything about it will be, and is, different from the franchise side of the business. Beginning with the jargon spoken and extending to accounting, if not properly managed, technology businesses can kill you quicker than a train. However, when it is done right your technology development might create a whole new revenue stream for you.

My advice is to bring in a consultant that can help you determine the best direction in this area early in the decision-making process.

The Ever Changing World of Technology

While I don't own a technology crystal ball, I can assure you of one thing – it will change and so must your brand's technology, if you are to stay in the game.

I believe technology will play a larger role in franchising in the next few years than it has in all previous years of franchise history. At no time has technology evolved as fast and furiously as mobile and online technology has in the last couple of years.

There was a recent article in Wired Magazine® that stated the Internet, as we know it, is dead. The article claimed that websites and browsing will migrate to a world of applications and dedicated connectivity, which means that the Internet will be a massive nerve system streaming information at incredible speeds. So what effect does this have on your franchise brand? A huge one actually.

Here are some technology areas that are starting to impact how we do franchising now:

- Cloud Computing
    - o We are moving away from centralized in-house servers and systems to an Internet cloud environment that provides storage, email, and other applications. If you are not exploring cloud computing for your company now you should be or you will be left in the dust.

- Mobile Applications
    - More and more companies are developing mobile applications for their franchise brands. A good example of this is the Great Clips® app that reports wait times for getting haircuts in their salons. You might want to start exploring apps for your concept.
- Mobile Content
    - Is your brand's website optimized for viewing on an iPhone®/smartphone or listed on Foursquare? If not, you're behind the curve already.
- Mobile Payments
    - Are your franchise locations equipped to accept mobile payments? Google Wallet and Square® are game changers and will impact your operations sooner than later. A key issue to remember with these new game changers is PCI compliance and the security of data.
- iPad® Menus
    - If you haven't ordered a meal or viewed a wine list on an iPad® yet don't worry, you will soon. If your franchisees are still carrying around clipboards, you have an iPad® application waiting to be developed.
- McTV
    - Call it gimmicky if you like but don't underestimate the power of digital TV or McDonald's®. Deploying localized digital TV into restaurants is nothing earth shattering at first blink, but if you virally interact with your customers through it by conducting polls, customer feedback, music, and other social connections, it is a big deal.

- Social Media
  - Just when you figure out one platform, along comes another. Social media is here to stay and you will need to stay abreast of it to compete both online and off.
- Twitter
  - Easy to dismiss, but more and more executives, including me, are using Twitter to communicate with peers. You need to pay attention to this movement and how it may play out for franchise development and customer interaction.

While some or all of these technology changes may have an effect on your brand at some point, the most important thing to remember is that <u>they will affect you</u>, <u>your brand</u>, and <u>how you do business</u>. There is no escaping the moving sands of technology.

Rule Summary

Let's face it, unless you're a geek like me, dealing with technology can be painful. Even for those of us that embrace it, things can go terribly wrong, but the bottom line is that in order to thrive as a franchise Mega-Brand, now and in the future, it has to be engrained into your company as a culture.

Key Points

- *Flatten out your IT department by "geek seeding" your departments, it will pay huge dividends.*
- *Don't kill your franchisee relationships with surprises in technology implementation and costs! Keep them involved in technology decisions.*
- *If you don't have one, put a technology policy in place.*

- *Systemwide technology implementation starts with a brand intranet.*
- *Develop "Just in Time Support" KPIs and dashboards.*
- *Keep your eye on technology changes and how it will affect your brand both short and long term.*

Continued from the beginning of the chapter:

Our ghost of technology past story picks up exactly where it left off – in the 90's. The average person might not notice, but Kmart® is still using the same heavy, bulky, IBM® POS systems they had in the 70's. There is a store near my home that I frequent and, not exaggerating, nearly every time I visit, the clerk has to reboot or has some difficulty with the POS system. How do you think Kmart's® information system stacks up to Walmart® or other competitors? It can't! If you haven't noticed, Kmart® has been struggling financially for many years. Do you wonder if their antiquated systems might have anything to do with it? I'm willing to bet it does. - *A past technology Mega-Wreck!*

Ghost of technology present... Andrew Grove, the past CEO of Intel® wrote a book titled, *Only the Paranoid Survive*. In it, he writes about "noise" or "buzz" that we hear as business people. As an example, at one time the Internet was just noise. We all had heard or read about it, knew very little about it, but understood that it might impact our business somehow.

Companies either react or ignore noise and the result can be a deflection point in their brand lifespan, meaning they gain from the noise or totally lose out on the change. For an example, did you know that early in the development of the Internet, Apple® Computer was the dominant player that handled Internet traffic? They chose to ignore it, lost their footing in that space and Cisco® took the advantage.

The noise that I reported to my Board of Directors about an Internet company that had created a disruptive business model in the computer repair break/fix model was real. Their business model commoditized computer repair by hosting an eBay®-style offering whereby companies needing services for computers allowed any technician to bid on it. Basically the cheapest most dependable basement or garage tech landed the job, driving down rates to unprofitable levels. Fortunately for our company, Expetec®, we had moved into a different technology sector and were not impacted by it as severely as other franchised, computer-repair chains were and still are today.

Pay attention to the noise. Look what disruptive Internet technologies have done to franchises in the travel, real estate, and other sectors. I repeat, "Pay attention to the noise." - *A present franchising technology Mega-Wreck caused by third party disruption!*

The ghost of technology future... I am going to step out on a limb here by making a prediction and by doing so, hope that I do not upset any of my friends in the franchised healthcare sector. In the beginning of the chapter I discussed the three camps of technology usage in this area: healthcare franchise brands using off-the-shelf software applications, brands that are using modified off-the-shelf software applications, and franchise brands that are developing cutting edge custom applications.

My prediction is that if you are a healthcare franchise system that is not developing proprietary custom software applications for your system, you may not be in a position to compete. My logic is straightforward: For the most part healthcare systems provide exactly the same service. You can argue that your methods of delivery, training, etc are different, but aside from those if you're using the same software platform as the brand down the street, what is your major competitive differentiator? See my point? Picture this, you are enthusiastically conducting a demo of your high-tech scheduling system to a prospective franchisee and they think, "Hmmm, this looks just like the software the other company that I looked at is using." Can this be avoided? Will the healthcare brands that invest heavily into proprietary software applications prevail? Only time will tell if my prediction comes true. - *A franchising technology Mega-Wreck that might happen!*

Rule No. 10 – Manage resources and understand the financial requirements to grow a franchise Mega-Brand.

"What's going to cost so much running a franchise company - why shouldn't I put the $30,000 in my pocket?" asked the young man sitting next to me at the roundtable I was facilitating.

By this time it was clear that what another experienced franchise executive and I had been telling this brand new franchisor for *30 minutes* had not sunk in at ANY level. He had recently sold his first franchisee and they had purchased three locations with a big fat check. We were desperately trying to get him to understand that he needed to bank the money because it was already earmarked for expenses he would be incurring in the near future, but he was too new to franchising and unable to accept this.

He had recently begun franchising a retail concept that featured tea-cup puppies of various breeds, showcased in baby cribs throughout the store. The year was 2009, and around the time that Paris Hilton was carrying a little dog around in her purse and was attracting lots of press and attention. His concept was based on the hype surrounding the growing sales of tea-cup puppies.

Now don't get me wrong, I am a "dog guy" and I love those cute little puppies (probably more than the average person). He was trying to build a business on a fad that didn't have much of a shelf life and he planned on sucking all the money out of the company. He had two seasoned C-level franchise executives, who had "been there - done that" telling him he was setting himself up for failure if he didn't heed our advice and that's what bothered me the most.

Later in the chapter, we'll check in with him to see if he took our advice and how he is doing today.

Company Capitalization Is Never A Cut And Dry Discussion because no two companies or circumstances are ever the same. However, there are certain rules concerning capitalization that can get you started in the right direction.

Let's begin by examining the basic lifecycle of franchise systems and their typical cash needs.

Traditional Franchise-System Lifecycles

Stage	Characteristics	Franchising Age
Development Stage	New concept and/or system with unpredictable franchise growth.	0 – 3 Years
Emerging Stage	Relatively new system with expanding infrastructure and unpredictable franchise growth.	3 – 6 Years
Mature Stage	Stabilized and predictable infrastructure and franchise growth.	Over 6 Years

Author's Note: For the purpose of this book, I am excluding company acquisitions, sector roll-up acquisitions, corporate owned locations expansion, fulfillment/supply chain management, large real estate needs, or other extraordinarily high capital requirements or growth initiatives. The lifecycle stages explained here are meant to address franchise operations and expansion in brands that have grown organically – by franchising not through acquisition, merger or equity investments.

The Development Stage of a Franchise Company

Franchising a concept is an expensive endeavor and failure to plan is a plan for failure.

Undercapitalization is the number one killer of any new business venture, whether or not it is franchised. It is vitally important that all new franchisors fully understand the cost of bringing a new brand to market *and* the amount of time it takes to do so. New franchise companies are unproven and have many unforeseen challenges and expenses, so the idea that you can cash flow through *initial franchise fees alone* is a fallacy.

In light of this, you must properly plan for cash needs through the first few years of growth until your company and system begin to stabilize. While it is entirely possible to "bootstrap" your growth, keep in mind that it will take considerably longer to grow to a sustainable size and the level of support your system requires will be compromised.

From my direct experience of creating seven franchise companies from scratch, I know that it will take an average of one year to **properly and completely** prepare a new franchise system for the "ready to launch" phase. This one-year timeframe assumes that you already have operating and profitable company locations or prototypes ready to replicate.

Franchise Mega-Brand's "Best of Class" at Startup Capitalization

P&G® - Agile Pursuits Franchising

Tide Dry Cleaners®
Mr. Clean Car Wash®

Owned and developed by the Proctor & Gamble Company (P&G), these two brands are certainly setup initially to become franchise Mega-Brands. Besides the level of capital that has been committed to these brands, P&G® spent years researching and massaging the "proof of concepts" before initial release to the public for expansion.

Both brands had a fair number of company owned locations open prior to franchise expansion.

However, if you do not have operating locations or operating locations making enough profits to cover the "5 Pennies" **and** provide a good return to a franchisee, you have no business starting a new franchise.

Proof of Concept *- Reasonably adequate profits for the franchisee must be met before you begin to franchise, or think of selling a franchise to anyone.*

In reading this statement, it may come across as being harsh, and it should. I cannot emphasize the importance of franchise profitability enough. It is the business and cultural essence that flows through every franchise Mega-Brand.

There may be some franchise "consultants" who try to convince you otherwise, but my advice is to steer away from those folks. No consultant with solid experience of operating franchises properly will overlook the seriousness of franchising a business. A good consultant will take all the time needed to help you get your franchising affairs properly in order to create a solid franchise offering.

In addition to the year of initial development, plan to take another couple of years to bring some normalcy to your franchise recruiting efforts and earned-royalty stream.

Because of the costs of initial development and the first few years of uncertain growth, you must plan on long-term cash flow needs of at least 3-4 years.

Although you will probably augment your cash flow with some initial franchise fees, counting on them to bank your sustainable growth could be disastrous and a mistake that could take your entire concept (including the franchisees who have invested into their money in the business) down.

Cash Burn Rate

A couple of good tools to help you plan for cash needs are the *cash burn rate* and the *cash zero date* of your company.

Cash burn rate, or negative cash flow as it is also called, is the capital used to finance your company's overhead/expenses before the company can cover them from adequate income. Cash burn rate is usually measured by the amount of cash spent per month and is best taken from an average spent over a period of time.

Spending can ebb and flow significantly during startup period and the averaging takes that into account. The longer the period you utilize to establish your burn rate, the better the established burn rate accuracy will be. For example, if you spent $180,000 over a six month period, your averaged cash burn rate would be $30,000 per month rounded off.

Take time to thoroughly analyze and project your company's cash. Remember to include larger capitalized purchases such as information systems and resale purchases such as inventory requirements, as both have an impact on cash flow needs.

Most companies that fail during startup fail because they underestimated their cash burn rate and worse yet, their cash zero date.

Cash Zero Date

Let me be the first one to say that "cash zero" is not a day anyone wants to see. It is effectively the date your company runs out of money and is the worst case scenario.

Why do you need to know this? Much like your cash burn rate, cash-zero date is a tool that gives you perspective on cash planning, and from my personal experience, you can never have enough tools for cash planning.

Let's face it, nobody wants to imagine their company running out of money, but the reality is that if you put a date on the calendar it keeps surprises from popping up and it makes for good business planning.

To calculate your cash-zero date, take your cash position on a given day and divide it by your average monthly burn rate.

Cash Zero Date Analysis

*Today's Date + (current cash / average monthly burn rate) =
Cash Zero Date*

Some companies will break it down even further by assuming there are 91 days in three working months and 364 working days per year. But to keep it simple, we are assuming a rounded off 30 day month.

For example, assume today is March 1, 2011 and you have $160,000 of cash in the bank. If your average monthly burn rate is $20,000, the calculation would come out as the following:

Cash Zero Date Working Analysis

March 1, 2011 + ($160,000 / $20,000) = November 1, 2011

or 8 months

It is important to emphasize that cash-zero date assumes there is no cash from operations coming in during that period. In the example above, if you generated $10,000 of income during this time frame, it would effectively change your cash-zero date to November 15, 2011.

If you have periodic cash coming in from operations, adjust your cash-zero date to reflect that. Maintain a current cash-zero date for the first few years of operation, or until the company finances began to smooth out.

Remember, cash-zero date is a worst-case scenario, but as a planning tool, it lets you know exactly where you are.

Development Cash Requirements

The cash requirements to create and launch a new franchise system can be broken down into three phases, each with distinct capital needs.

Initial Capital Planning Phases

Development Phase	Expenditure Item	Low Estimate	High Estimate
Phase 1 - Strategic Franchise-Brand Planning	Strategic Franchise Brand Planning	$10,000	$30,000
Phase 2 - Initial Concept Development	Franchise System Creation & Development	$75,000	$150,000
Phase 3 - Growth Capital	Initial Growing of the System	$25,000	$200,000
Total		**$110,000**	**$380,000**

Author's Note: *These estimates are based upon franchising a pre-existing proven concept.*

Phase 1 – Strategic Franchise-Brand Planning

U.S. Lawns®, a commercial landscape management company based in Orlando, FL, is a franchise Mega-Brand that has been franchising since 1986. Much of U.S. Lawns® success can be attributed directly to their initial strategic plan that was based on locally-owned offices. Their strategy proved then and now that local franchisees can create and foster deeper relationships with large property accounts than U.S. Lawns® could using corporate staff.

A strategic franchise plan is the most important step in building a new franchise company and it should not be rushed. Developing one can take a few days or a few years, depending on the complexity of the brand.

Many new franchisors and large corporations make the key mistake of starting with the legal and marketing aspects of the franchise before they completely understand how the system could or should operate. The legal documents and franchise marketing materials are necessary to sell franchises and grow your system, but they should be developed after you have determined, through successfully running proof-of-concept units, that franchising your concept is feasible and you have a *solid strategy* with which do it.

Franchising is an alternative distribution system for existing products and services and must be thought of and planned for accordingly. There are too many options that must be fleshed out before any money is paid to a reputable law firm to create a Franchise Disclosure Document (FDD).

Many factors need to be considered when developing a strategic franchise plan including a feasibility study, unit replication and opening requirements, unit support requirements, training needs, franchise expansion models, royalty structures, advertising and marketing, infrastructure needs, information systems analysis, real estate, supply chain management, internal and external SWOT (Strength, Weakness, Opportunity, Threat) analyses, competitive analysis and benchmarking, intellectual property protection, franchisee profiling, financial modeling, corporate structure, and much more.

After a thorough analysis of your concept is done compile the information into a comprehensive, strategic, franchise-business plan which is then distilled to a shorter, executive, strategic-franchise plan that is less than ten pages long. This will serve as your foundation and roadmap to creating and growing your system.

Phase 2 – Franchise System Creation & Development

Armed with your executive, strategic-franchise plan you're now ready to begin the hard work to pull it all together.

Much of your strategic planning session ideas will become projects, taking on lives of their own. A Gantt chart is a very useful tool that I've used extensively for managing multiple projects and keeping a new brand on course.

Creating a Gantt chart not only helps you identify the relevant projects that need to be completed, but it creates priorities and timelines for doing so. As you populate your Gantt chart, you will see a graphic representation of your expected launch date and the beginning of Phase 3, the initial growth of your franchise system.

Development Gantt Chart Example

Item	Month	Month	Month	Month	Month	Month
Franchisee Training Agenda		███	███	███		
Operations Manual Creation	███	███	███	███		
FDD Creation	███	███	███			
Financial Audit	███	███				
Build New Website			███	███		
Brand Launch						███

Author's Note: *For illustrative purposes, this Gantt chart represents a sampling of items required to create and launch a franchise brand.*

Depending on the complexity of your franchise concept, the project list on your Gantt chart could be quite lengthy. Create a new Gantt chart for any projects that contain many sub-items, otherwise, your main Gantt chart will get too large to manage. In my experience is the simpler you keep your Gantt charts, the better off you are.

No two concepts are the same so the project lists will always vary, but there are core elements that must be developed for any franchise company.

The following table represents many of the items that you must address and complete prior to launching your new franchise.

Phase 2 – Franchise System Creation & Development Items

Franchise Operations & Other Required Manuals	New Franchisee Training Agenda & Materials	Determining Legal Counsel (FDD & Trademark Filing)	Franchise Disclosure Document (FDD)
Franchisee Support Systems	Franchisee Intranet & Communications	Store/Unit Information Systems (POS)	Real Estate Selection
Suppliers & Purchasing	Construction Plans & Options	Store Signage	Store Load Out & Merchandising
Websites, eCommerce, & Internet Marketing Strategies	Quality Assurance	Franchisee Field Support	Franchisee Marketing & Advertising
Public Relations	New Franchisee Marketing Materials	Franchise Compliance & Policies	Franchisee Relations & Policies
New Franchisee	Internal Staff	System Metrics	New Franchisee

Profile	Franchise Training	& Management	Recruiting Process

Author's Note: *Core franchise elements listed only. Always employ a reputable franchise consultant with brand management experience to assist you in developing your franchise offering and brand-specific requirements.*

If franchising is a new endeavor for you, I highly recommend retaining the services of a franchise consultant with previous brand management experience to assist you with your franchise modeling and creation. Their expertise and guidance will save you time, money, and countless headaches.

Phase 3 – Initial Growing of the System

Ready… Set… Now what do you do?

So you've managed to get your franchise concept ready for launch and are now wondering where all the buyers are - right?

Most new franchisors head straight to the Internet and start spending big bucks on franchise advertising portals. Unfortunately many new franchisors blow their entire advertising budget on randomly picked portals and have zero results to show for it. In some instances, I have seen new franchise companies hit their cash-zero date before they sold *any* franchises.

Franchise development has become a science and to avoid this problem I suggest reading an excellent "how to" book about Phase 3 growing and selling your franchise called *Grow to Greatness* by Steve Olson.

In *Grow to Greatness*, Steve writes about the necessary steps to establish a high-performance franchise-recruiting process including creating a development team that will get your new franchise Mega-Brand out of the gates and growing.

The Emerging-Stage Franchise Company

As kids reach their teenage years they struggle between the worlds of being a kid and facing adult issues, decisions, and responsibilities. Through that period of their life some of them rebel, some of them glide right through, and many bounce through with high drama.

Franchise companies that have grown beyond the first few years of startup often behave like teenagers going through those turbulent times. Your company will require money for this, money for that and may seem to fight you at times - just like a teenager!

Emerging-stage franchise companies typically are not quite at the point where they have royalty self-sufficiency, defined as enough royalty income to cover the operating costs, let alone any infrastructure expansion needs. This creates the challenge of balancing the cash needs between a growing infrastructure and a new franchisee acquisition budget or lack thereof. It's like the chicken and the egg story; In order to fund your infrastructure needs you must sell franchises, and to sell franchises you must spend money on advertising. So which gets the money first, the infrastructure or the advertising?

Franchise Mega-Brand's "Best of Quotes" on Growth-Capital Needs

"In the early years, I didn't understand or plan for the infrastructure needs that the company required. Because of that, I had many near-death experiences from a lack of cash. Many times I was concerned about making payroll! New and emerging franchisors must make cash plans beyond the first fifty franchise units. We were very lucky!

– Fred DeLuca, President and Co-Founder, SUBWAY® Restaurants

Budgeting & Departmentalization

I have heard the question *"How can I budget money that I don't have?"*

It seems sometimes that there is no other cure for a cash shortage than more of it. While this may be true when you have payroll on Friday and not enough cash to cover it, there are ways to help avoid the catastrophe. In addition to your cash-burn rate and cash-zero date analyses, there are other good tools that can help manage the available cash and its allocation: detailed budgeting, employee incentives and departmental allocations.

Detailed budgeting should be used from day one. To effectively use a budget develop three different versions – high, medium, and low. Switch between versions to meet the company's needs and ensure viability based on current sales and cash flow.

Going from a low budget to a high budget can mean additional staff, increased advertising, etc. The reverse effect could mean staff reductions and decreased spending activities.

Budget Types

Budget Versions/Cash Burn Rate	Budget Purpose
Low	Also known as the "keeping the lights on" budget. This plan calls for the least amount of resources and cash burn required to stay in business.
Medium	The "normal operating" budget, which also accounts for some moderate growth investment.
High	A "growth acceleration" budget that steps up growth investment, but still retains/builds cash reserves for future uncertainty.

Creating budgets and adhering to them requires staff discipline and tight internal controls and processes. These controls and processes include purchase orders and requests, inventory control and travel authorizations.

Bonus plans are another useful tool to ensure your staff adheres to the current budget. Bonus plans are linked to budgetary requirements. For example, you might establish an annual or quarterly staff bonus for staying within the budget or identifying further cost reductions. Individual staff member's bonus amounts can be adjusted based upon their ability to influence the budget in their given work area.

Consider using non-cash rewards such as a company cookout, hotel coupons for a free stay, restaurant gift cards or other incentives for reaching budget goals. Regardless of how you bonus your staff, they will begin to pay more attention to the spending habits of the company when their rewards are attached to budget performance. That is a good thing!

It is important to break your business into departments. Some people may think that departments only apply to large corporations, but if you have only one staff member providing a function within your company, it can be assigned or designated as a department. Departmentalization allows you to divide individual pieces of the business operations such as franchise development, accounting, training, support, real estate, marketing, IT, and other functions into smaller manageable pieces.

The information gleaned from departmentalizing can astonish you and, in some cases, the numbers may show a reason to outsource certain functions rather than doing it in-house. For example, with the availability of cloud computing and online IT services, very few companies need an in-house IT staff unless it is supporting proprietary equipment or software needs for franchisees.

An accurate, departmentalized view of your IT costs will allow you to contrast those costs to outsourced services in order to make an informed management decision.

Rent, utilities, phone, general overhead, etc should be uniformly applied to each department based on a determined percentage of use per department. In order to determine the percentage factor, assess costs in a variety of ways including percentage of total useable base used or per person in each department. To get an accurate cost of your franchise development department, include the total cost of acquiring new franchisees. To account for all costs for franchise development you will need to approach it holistically by including marketing and advertising for new franchisees, contact management systems and other franchise development specific costs.

Cost Per New Franchisee

A great byproduct of departmentalizing is a number that you absolutely must know to effectively run a franchise company is "cost per new franchisee" for each new unit sold.

To calculate "cost per new franchisee" divide the total annual cost of your franchise development department including labor, expenses, marketing, advertising, contact management, and other costs by the number of new franchises sold that year.

Cost per New Franchisee Analysis

Total Annual Franchise Development Dept Expense / # of new franchisees sold per year = Cost per New Franchisee

To illustrate, if you spend $200,000 per year and recruit ten new franchisees, your cost per new franchisee would be $20,000. If your current franchise fee is $15,000 and your cost per new franchisee is $20,000, you would be going backwards in cash flow $5,000 every time a new owner joins the team.

The negative cash flow of $5,000 doesn't include any financing you might provide, broker fees, initial training costs or support costs to launch the new franchisee. In this scenario these additional costs would significantly increase your negative cash flow. So the more locations you sell, the faster you go broke!

As this illustrates, an incorrectly computed franchise fee could have a significant negative impact on your company's cash flow. An experienced franchise consultant who sets up your franchise business should model these costs when setting your initial franchise fee. If your cost per new franchisee is too high in relation to a reasonable, competitive franchise fee, you must re-evaluate your costs or have adequate cash reserves to offset the negative cash flow.

Too many companies establish their initial fees based solely upon their competitors' or other franchise companies' fees and not based on their own costs and needs. Don't be afraid to make adjustments to your initial franchise fee when needed. Before adjusting your fees consult with your legal counsel about the impact this change will have on your FDD. Adjusting your franchise fee is considered a "material change" to your FDD that requires you to update your state registrations and re-disclose any potential franchise candidates you are currently working with.

A Seasoned Set of Eyes

I had a discussion with Fred DeLuca, the President and Co-Founder of SUBWAY® Restaurants concerning emerging franchise companies. He indicated that after startup it took him nine years to figure out the sandwich business and another nine years to figure out the franchise business. If you do the math, it took him 18 years to figure out the business.

Unfortunately, when Fred created SUBWAY® Restaurants in 1965 there weren't many of the resources available for franchising that there are today. Back then new franchisors had to learn by bloodying their knees. Fred's suggestion for all franchisors today is to take advantage of the resources and get expert help and advice!

With so many moving pieces during this crazy emerging phase of your company, it is strongly recommended to have an experienced C-Level franchise executive spend some time assessing your system. Choose someone who has dealt with these issues first-hand, because they will have the experience to spot any looming problems and advise you on best options for continued growth.

As the old saying goes, "You don't know what you don't know!" Don't let that get in your way of being a franchise Mega-Brand.

The Mature-Stage Franchise Company

Attend any franchise-specific events and you will hear the word "brand" used frequently.

When a franchise company reaches a certain scope and size the "brand" begins to mature, emerge and gain some name recognition. This stage is often referred to as "hitting critical mass".

As the company attains critical mass and grows, its capital requirements become more predictable and its budgets become a normal part of the daily operation. As a result, management's attention typically starts to shift towards maximizing shareholder return and seeking strategic growth opportunities. Growth opportunities can range from building your current brand to starting or acquiring a second franchise brand.

Franchise Mega-Brand's "Best of Class" at Multi-Brand Management

The Dwyer Group

Mr. Rooter®
Mr. Electric®
Glass Doctor®
Rainbow International®
Mr. Appliance®
Aire Serv®
The Grounds Guys®

Founded by Don Dwyer in 1981, The Dwyer Group has grown from its original brand Rainbow International to seven franchise brands with over 1,400 locations worldwide.

Led by CEO and Chairwoman Dina Dwyer-Owens, The Dwyer Group believes new franchise owners are attracted to the company's franchise opportunities because of the commitment to the company's mission, vision and Code of Values; the established reputation of its management team and the success of its franchise systems.

Scaling to Multiple Brands

If you are starting or acquiring a second brand it is paramount that your expansion efforts do not *negatively impact* your existing brand in any way. When the expansion of the second brand is properly planned, it will enhance the current brand economically by decreasing expenses through economies of scale and by providing additional unit-expansion opportunities for existing franchisees.

Much like the first franchise brand was before it grew to produce positive results; the second brand will have all the capital needs that impacted the initial brand.

When making the decision to move forward with a second brand you must consider "autonomous" or "integrated operations" options. Because every company has different circumstances, operations, resources, etc. your structure should be determined by what makes the best sense for your company's current situation and strategic growth objectives.

Autonomous Operations

Choosing the best structure is dependent upon the circumstances surrounding your expansion. When you acquire an existing franchise company, depending on the strength of its operations, geographic location, etc., it may make sense to let it run autonomously. This will cause the least disruption to the acquired company's culture and staff.

Over time the finances of the accounting, franchise development, marketing departments and other operational functions can be examined and integrated into the existing company's departments to decrease expenses and increase efficiencies.

Certain companies or entities such as private equity firms and investor pools, typically choose to allow their investments to run autonomously because they are in the business of investing in companies, rather than operating companies.

Again, the decision in selecting the type of structure for the second brand must also include the options that make the most operational sense for your company.

Integrated Operations

When you are launching or acquiring a new brand or are a non-franchised company that expands into franchising as a distribution model, all your existing company's operational functions should be evaluated to determine which ones will, or can provide services to the new franchise entity.

To help determine this, break your company's operations into two categories: those that are brand-specific and those that are not.

Training, field support, and franchise development are usually brand-specific and tend to be difficult to integrate because those departments are very focused on operational specialties and it is challenging to apply the nuances of a new brand into current operations. Integration can be eventually accomplished by creating larger training, field support, and franchise development departments and assigning an executive to oversee brand-specific teams.

In some cases brand-specific operations are so unique that they need to remain as autonomous departments.

Franchise Mega-Brand's "Best of Class" at Private Equity Franchise Acquisition and Integration

Roark Capital Group

Carvel®
Seattle's Best®
Cinnabon®
Schlotsky's®
Moe's®
Auntie Anne's®
Batteries Plus®
FASTSIGNS®
McAlister's Deli®
Money Mailer®
Primrose Schools®
Pet Valu®
Bosley's®
Wingstop®

Roark Capital Group is an Atlanta-based private equity firm with more than $1.5 billion in equity capital under management. Roark has acquired 25 businesses from the entrepreneurs who founded them or their families, and prides itself on being a trusted financial partner for management and business owners.

Accounting, marketing, public relations, and information technology, are all examples of departments and services that are scalable in a multi-brand environment and should be evaluated for possible integration.

Economies of scale can decrease expenses and increase productivity so any opportunity to integrate departments and services should be evaluated and considered. Caution! , Don't get trapped by the math alone in your quest for efficiencies. Current franchisee support or franchise relations must not be compromised in favor of gaining a dollar! It is short-sighted and most likely will have a negative impact on the brand. So while it might make sense, mathematically, to integrate a function, you have to look at the bigger picture and do what's right for your franchisees! Keep in mind that your current franchisees are your best emissaries. They are viewed by prospects as a window into the franchisor's practices. Unhappy franchisees will negatively influence prospects.

Multi-Brand Advantages

I am a huge proponent of multi-brand franchise systems because of the economies of scale that they afford and the competitive advantages that come with them.

One advantage is revenue balance. With multiple brands, when sales are up 5% in one brand and down 3% in another, your company still maintains a 2% sales increase when viewed on a consolidated, financial statement. This diversification helps not only the franchisor, but its franchisees too. They benefit because the franchisor remains financially healthy and has the resources to invest in the system.

Purchasing and distribution is a direct benefit to the franchisees. The greater the number of franchise units, the greater the buying power. This represents lower costs and increased profits for franchisees. Increased purchasing power also leads to greater supply chain efficiencies because the increased volume produces a reduction in distribution costs.

Two franchise Mega-Brands that excel with multi-brands and have been highlighted in this section are The Dwyer Group in Waco, TX and Roark Capital Group, a private equity firm located in Atlanta, GA. In my opinion both of these companies represent how multi-brands should be developed and managed. From The Dwyer Group's incredible culture and unit profitability, to Roark Capital Group's integration prowess, best practices sharing and implementation – these are two companies you can study on how to do it right.

A Word on Partners and Investors

Nothing can derail a solid franchise plan faster than investors or partners that neither understand franchising nor grasp the "end-customer business" that you are in.

If you are seeking financial partners or investors, they must understand that it takes time to grow a franchise system and that the "riches" of franchising are NOT the franchise fees. Unfortunately, some investors are drawn to the franchising because they see large franchise fees being charged and inaccurately compare them to a non-franchised company's normal sales.

Another danger sign is misconceptions about the "end customer business".

Can you imagine the disaster you would have if a large bread-baking company financially partnered with a sub-sandwich chain with the end goal of selling the franchisees more bread at an escalated price? Not only would the franchisees' purchasing costs get out of control, but stores could close, you would receive a lot of nasty phone calls and lawsuits would follow closely behind. This is what happens when buyers and investors fail to understand the "end customer business."

Franchisees want an efficient system with the best profit margins, not one that makes more money at the expense of its franchisees.

The bottom line: When you are busy battling your investors, you cannot keep your eye on the growth and support of your franchisees.

When I was raising money for a new franchise brand, a friend of mine once told me, *"Don't be blinded by the money, be sure the deal is good and makes sense first."*

Having experienced this firsthand, I know that seeing a whole bunch of zeros behind a big number is very enticing. However, complete your due diligence on prospective partners and be sure that there isn't a higher price to pay than the term sheet specifies. I am not saying that investors who have never been involved in franchising wouldn't make a good partner, but I am recommending that you consider the time and energy you will spend educating them.

And oh by the way... Have your investors read this book - it will save you many headaches!

Rule Summary

You have probably figured out by now that franchising is pretty serious business. The masters of growing and operating franchise Mega-Brands realize that a vibrant franchisor equals a vibrant system.

Managing the human, operating, and capital resources of any size franchise company is hard work and the needs of your system can change quickly as the number of units increase.

I'll never forget a conversation I had with a guy that was considering creating a new franchise concept. As I was telling him about a franchise company's infrastructure concerning legal, staff, capital, field support, training, length of time to create and so forth, he stopped me mid-sentence and said "Really? I didn't realize that a franchise was like a real company and needed all of that. I just thought you could put up a website and start selling franchises."

I wish I could remember his name - I'd send him a copy of *Five Pennies*.

Key Points

- *Keep an eye on the cash – it is your lifeblood.*
- *Identify which lifecycle of franchising you are in and the cash requirements for it.*
- *Proof of concept – have one!!*
- *Formulate your system growth based on your strategic franchise plan.*
- *Sometimes a seasoned set of eyes is needed to stay on course.*
- *Have the right partners.*
- *Franchise your business for the right reason as the others will bring destruction to your concept, legacy, and finances.*

Continued from the beginning of the chapter:

OK, now back to the guy with the puppy franchise. The last I heard he wasn't doing so well and ended up selling or giving the entire franchise company to the very person who wrote the $30,000 check. - *A franchising Mega-Wreck!*

Ten Rules Pocket Summary

- **Rule No. 1 - Tee up your franchisees for mega-success, not failure!**

  Show your commitment to sustainable franchisee unit profitability by adopting this as your new brand strategic statement, "Our wealth and success as a franchisor will be a by-product of developing wealthy and successful franchisees."

- **Rule No. 2 – Franchising is a mega-relationship business!**

  Foster a culture of positive franchisee relations and codependency. Remember - developing a culture of great franchisee engagement and relations doesn't happen overnight. It takes time, a consistent championing by leadership, a ton of hard work, and a commitment to constant system improvement.

- **Rule No. 3 – Franchising is not a drag race, it is more like the 24 hours of Daytona.**

  Stay ahead of your growth! Remember that building a successful franchise system is a race of endurance - not speed, and that fast track growth without proper planning or execution will cause significant problems that may, or may not, be able to be resolved.

- **Rule No. 4 – Do not have an accountant remove a brain tumor!**

  Develop a culture of continuous improvement and franchise education throughout the entire organization. Remember that next to undercapitalization - a lack of franchising experience and knowledge is a top reason why some franchise systems fail.

- **Rule No. 5 - Plant, cultivate, and harvest system best practices.**

  Create a best practices clock of continuous unit improvement that cascades tools, resources, programs, and efficiencies back to the entire system.

- **Rule No. 6 - Stack the "entire" deck with strong franchise owners.**

  Remember the goal of recruiting is to minimize the risk of an incompatible owner and increase the acceptance of potential superstars by establishing a desirable profile and "awarding franchises" to those that meet it.

- **Rule No. 7 - Focus on where "the rubber hits the racetrack."**

  Never lose site that royalties are earned when the franchisee cash register rings. Develop a relentless focus on supporting store operations and driving sales.

- **Rule No. 8 - Create partners in growth.**

  Create "something more" for your franchisees and brand by developing growth programs and/or tools that positively impact the entire system such as national partnerships, accounts, or other macro-level programs.

- **Rule No. 9 - Manage your system like NASA would.**

  Invest in technology that will keep your brand at the front of the pack. Maintain an eye on technology changes and how it will affect your brand both short and long term.

- **Rule No. 10 – Manage resources and understand the financial requirements to grow a franchise Mega-Brand.**

  Remember that a vibrant franchisor equals a vibrant system. Diligently manage the human, operating, and capital resources of your franchise system to ensure that you can make changes quickly.

Selected Bibliography

Books & Publications

Anderson, Mac and Feltenstein, Tom, *Change is Good... You go First.* (Illinois: Simple Truths, 2007).

Bloom, Bruce V., Nelson, Steve, and Franchise Relations Committee, *Improved Communications Means Improved Franchise Relations.* (District of Columbia: International Franchise Association, 2003)

Collins, James C., *Good to Great: Why some companies make the leap... and others don't* (New York: Harper Collins, 2001).

[1] Super 8 Motel's® Superline® and V.I.P Club data provided by: El-Hai, Jack, *Clean and Friendly for More Than 25 Years* (Connecticut: Greenwich Publishing Group, Inc., 1999)

Grove, Andrew S., *Only the Paranoid Survive: How to Exploit the Crisis Points That Challenge Every Company.* (New York: Crown Publishing Group, 1999)

Harnish, Verne, *Mastering the Rockefeller Habits* (New York: SelectBooks, 2002).

Morgan Stanley, *Internet Trends Study* (June, 2010)

Olson, Steve, *Grow to Greatness: How to build a world-class franchise system faster.* (California: Franchise Update Media Group, 2008)

Sun, Shelly, *Grow Smart, Risk Less: A Low Capital Path to Multiplying Your Business Through Franchising.* (Texas: Greenleaf Book Group Press, 2011)

About the Author

Lonnie Helgerson, CFE

CEO, Author, Speaker & Serial Frantrepreneur!

Lonnie has over 27 years in the franchise industry working with companies such as Super 8 Motels®, Ident-A-Kid®, and many more.

Recognized as the pioneer in the mobile computer service franchise sector, Lonnie was the founder of Computer Doctor® the first franchise of its kind and two other technology franchise chains; Expetec® Technology Services & InstantFX Web Services. From 2006 - 2009, Lonnie was President and Chief Operations Officer of Ident-A-Kid Services of America® the largest child safety franchise in the United States.

He is currently CEO of Helgerson Franchise Group, a platform company that owns and operates franchise brands. In addition, Helgerson Franchise Group provides outsourced franchise services for new, emerging, and mature franchise systems.

Lonnie has served on many boards and committees including two-term Chairman, VetFran committee, International Franchise Association; the Institute of Certified Franchise Executives Board of Governors; International Franchise Association Franchisor Forum; Board of Advisors at The International Institute of Franchise Education, H. Wayne Huizenga School of Business and Entrepreneurship, Nova Southeastern University; and Board of Directors of the Franchisor Association of Florida.

He is a frequent speaker and facilitator for the International Franchise Association, Franchisor Association of Florida and many other various franchise and business seminars. He has also served as a member of the Board of Advisors for the Institute of Franchise Management graduate school, University of St. Thomas, Minneapolis, MN and is a three time graduate of their

MBA program for Franchise Management. In 2002 he became a designated CFE (Certified Franchise Executive).

In addition to *Five Pennies*, Lonnie is also the published author of *Buying a Franchise - Is it Right for Me?*

Throughout his career, Lonnie has been featured or written about in many books, magazines, newspapers, TV and radio including the national college textbook Small Business Management, USA Today, Wall Street Journal, Entrepreneur Magazine, CNBC Squawk Box, Your World with Neil Cavuto and Paul Harvey.

Lonnie and his wife Linette reside in sunny Florida with their four beautiful children Chandler, Ainsley, Hannah, and Nora.

Index